LATINAS AND LATINOS ON TV

Latinx Pop Culture

SERIES EDITORS

Frederick Luis Aldama and Arturo J. Aldama

LATINAS AND LATINOS ON TV

Colorblind Comedy in the Post-Racial Network Era

Isabel Molina-Guzmán

THE UNIVERSITY OF
ARIZONA PRESS

TUCSON

The University of Arizona Press
www.uapress.arizona.edu

ISBN-13: 978-0-8165-3724-2 (paper)

Cover design by Leigh McDonald

Publication of this book is made possible in part by the proceeds of a permanent endowment created with the assistance of a Challenge Grant from the National Endowment for the Humanities, a federal agency.

Library of Congress Cataloging-in-Publication Data
Names: Molina-Guzmán, Isabel, author.
Title: Latinas and Latinos on TV : colorblind comedy in the post-racial network era / Isabel Molina-Guzmán.
Description: Tucson : The University of Arizona Press, 2018. | Series: Latinx pop culture | Includes bibliographical references and index.
Identifiers: LCCN 2017042857 | ISBN 9780816537242 (pbk. : alk. paper)
Subjects: LCSH: Hispanic Americans on television. | Situation comedies (Television programs)—United States.
Classification: LCC PN1992.8.H54 M65 2018 | DDC 791.45/652968073—dc23 LC record available at https://lccn.loc.gov/2017042857

Printed in the United States of America
♾ This paper meets the requirements of ANSI/NISO Z39.48-1992 (Permanence of Paper).

Por las cuatro cámaras de mi corazón

Luciano, Ian, Rafael y Isabel Luciana

CONTENTS

ILLUSTRATIONS

ACKNOWLEDGMENTS

This book has been percolating in my head since 2010 when then-PhD candidate Shantel Martinez invited me to think about the cultural politics of space in *Modern Family*, a show we both watched and cautiously enjoyed. I thank Dr. Martinez for asking me to reflect on the racial and class logics of space on the show that would become the backbone of this project's analysis. Without funding from the Department of Media and Cinema Studies for leave, this book would not have been written. Funding from the Illinois Campus Research Board provided me with the ability to work with the amazing student scholars in the Institute of Communications Research. Bryce Henson and Kerry Wilson conducted some of the data collection. Kerry also tracked down obscure references and provided copyediting assistance. Morten Kristensen worked the longest and most intensely on this project—from the early stages of annotated bibliographies to the final drafts—and this book would not exist without the thoughtful conversations I had with him throughout the researching and writing of this book.

Barbie Zelizer, Emily Plowman, and the faculty and students at the Annenberg School for Communication provided me with an invaluable semester as a visiting scholar. The intellectual exchanges and conversations I had with colleagues there were central to the book's final revisions. Latina/o studies powerhouse duo Drs. Arturo and Frederick Aldama believed in this book from the start, and it is their commitment to contemporary Latina/o culture and scholarship that enabled its publication. Fede, I am forever grateful for the continuing support you provide all of your colleagues working in this area. I am particularly appreciative of Kristen Buckles at the University of Arizona Press, who advocated for this series and took a chance on this format. Both Kristen and Stacey Wujcik waited patiently for the revisions and carefully saw this book through production. The entire editorial team at the University of Arizona Press got the book, and I am particularly grateful for their professionalism and editorial support.

In 2012 Diana Negra, co-editor of *Gendering the Recession: Media and Culture in an Age of Austerity*, asked if I was working on the show

Modern Family and invited me to write about it for the collection. Her excellent editorial guidance and probing questions forced me to take the show and its political economic context seriously, and I am grateful for the privilege of working out some of the ideas that would shape this book with her. My conversations and academic engagement with scholars Sarah Banet-Weiser, Jillian Báez, Vicki Mayer, and Angharad Valdivia challenged me to rethink my assumptions about production practices, representation, and reception. I am particularly indebted to Angharad who has played the role of mentor and sage since my days as an undergraduate at Penn State. Without her pioneering work to create the intellectual field of Latino communication studies, this book could not have been possible. Angharad is part of a cohort of interdisciplinary feminist and ethnic studies scholars at the University of Illinois at Urbana-Champaign that opened up scholarly pathways that had not existed at key moments in my career. My personal and professional relationships with writers and scholars such as Angharad, David Coyoca, Karen Flynn, Soo Ah Kwon, Mimi Nguyen, and Fiona Ngo shaped this book. However, if there is one person who has transformed my academic development as an interdisciplinary communications scholar, it is Lisa Marie Cacho. My conversations with her and David are filled with laughter and lots of food and wine (at least for me) but never any dullness. Lisa's sharp insights into ethnicity, race, inequality, and culture shape my teaching and research in countless ways. Her intellectual energy is always with me, asking me to be clearer in my thoughts, more nuanced in my analysis, and more particular about the words I choose and scholars I cite. Thank you, Lisa, for being part of my personal and intellectual life.

Finally, my sisters, Michele and Joana, and nephew, Brady, kept my feet on the ground and my cultural references up to date with their patient love for the absent-minded professor in the family. And my *ositos* (Isabel Luciana and Rafael) nurtured the *mamoni* in me, literally taking care of me when I physically and emotionally needed it. They lovingly and happily provided unlimited Chano sitting. During the writing of this book, we welcomed our "sky baby" Luciano Hermann Molina-Sprandel into our life. It is my hope for a better future for him and others that sustains my academic work. I am blessed in every moment I share with you, Luciano, and Dada, your father, my life stone and husband, Ian Tyson Sprandel. Ian, you patiently keep me whole (and yes, well fed) and have never wavered in your unconditional support for all my sane and not-so-sane endeavors. I dedicate my labor to you and our family, and I give you my unwavering love in return.

All of the strengths of this book belong to my intellectual community of scholars, family, and friends. All the limitations are mine alone.

LATINAS AND LATINOS
ON TV

INTRODUCTION

Latina/os, Hipster Racism, and Post-Racial TV

Colorblindness is inherently seductive in a well-intentioned society full of liberal guilt, one that can then avail itself of certain legal discourses, for instance justice is blind and thus objective and fair.

KRISTEN WARNER

Since ABC's *George Lopez* left the airwaves in 2007 as the only network show with a Latino lead, the representational fortunes of Latina/o actors shifted away from media invisibility and toward an era of increasing inclusion.[1] Sofía Vergara became the highest-paid woman and Latina on TV through her starring role on *Modern Family* (2009–Present). In the first successful dramedy starring a Latina since ABC's *Ugly Betty* (2006–10), Gina Rodriguez gained critical acclaim for her role on the CW's *Jane the Virgin* (2014–Present). And the first Latina leading lady of TV, America Ferrera (*Ugly Betty*), returned to TV stardom in NBC's *Superstore* (2015 Present). These programs all came of age within TV's post-network era, an era television studies scholar Amanda Lotz (2004) defines by the digitalization of TV technology, ubiquity of mobile and on-demand technologies, and a seemingly limitless number of niche cable networks. This period of diversity in casting allowed U.S. Latina/o lives and culture to be front and center, yet a careful look at TV comedic content and production reveals a more troubling terrain for Latina/o producers, writers, actors, and audiences. Decades of work by activists in the Multi-Ethnic Media Coalition made the top five TV networks (ABC, CW, Fox, CBS, NBC) accountable for the lack of diversity in front of and behind the TV screen, and as a result, Latina/o faces became more prevalent on scripted TV. But the roles and storylines that surround comedic Latina/o characters have remained constrained by TV's ideological and economic demands for colorblindness. By

3

colorblindness I am referring to the belief that skin color or other physical markers of racial or ethnic identity are irrelevant.

Beginning with the Golden Age of 1950s TV, primetime comedies, also known as sitcoms, have played a significant cultural role for U.S. and global audiences.[2] Historically, the narratives and plots of most TV comedies center on the celebration of the norms and values of Judeo-Christian beliefs, middle-class whiteness, and heterosexual family structures through feel-good storytelling (Morreale 2003). Traditional sitcom storylines and the ideological messages communicated through them, especially in family sitcoms, focus on the importance of familial relationships, be they biological or chosen. Primetime sitcom storylines and characters rarely critique the underlying white privilege that inform the genre's characters and narrative conventions. Contemporary sitcoms, even those starring or featuring Latina/o and other ethnic-racial minority actors, maintain the conservative ideological drive of the genre (Mock 2011). In this book, I explore the role of ethnicity, race, and gender in primetime comedies that featured Latina/o actors and characters through the periodic framework of the *post-racial era of TV*. To do so I analyze the roles of Latina/o actors in multicultural ensemble casts on 22-minute comedies, specifically *Modern Family* (2009–Present), *The Office* (2005–13), *Scrubs* (2001–10), *Parks and Recreation* (2009–15), *Telenovela* (2015–16), and *Superstore* (2015–Present). The format of the 22-minute comedy has changed dramatically from the days of three-camera studio sitcoms such as *Friends* (1994–2004), but it remains one of the most enduring, successful, and profitable genres on U.S. TV (Mills 2008; Morreale 2003).

The Post-Racial TV Era

The comedies examined are among the most lucrative in terms of audience demographics, ratings, syndication, and, consequently, advertising revenue (Cantor 2014). These shows also came into existence and declined or gained in audience popularity during a significant historical, cultural, and political period for the United States (2007–16): the 2008 presidential campaign, the eight-year presidency of Barack H. Obama, and the subsequent election of Donald J. Trump, a period I label the post-racial era of U.S.-produced television.

Journalists and political pundits heralded Obama's 2008 election as a sign of the U.S. voting population's colorblindness—empirical proof that the nation's citizens had finally moved beyond seeing race and discriminating against racial difference. Reflecting on the final years of Obama's presidency, the opposite of that popular observation was clearly true. Likewise, post-racial TV celebrates the visibility of ethnic-racial difference and moves away from stereotypes. At the same time, post-racial productions operate under the assumption that audiences no longer see racial difference and are past racial discrimination—subscribing to the post-racial belief that TV's comedic texts and the audiences who watch them are now colorblind.

Peter Kuryla (2011) notes the following about the conservative ethos of colorblind discourse under the Obama presidency: "In the public square the phrase 'colour blind' operates today largely as a conservative rebuke of race-based initiatives proposed and endorsed by American liberals and leftists" (122–23). Colorblind legal and political discourses presume Civil Rights era policies, such as affirmative action, interfere with the free marketplace of ideas and competition that define the United States as a liberal democratic capitalist econ omy. Indeed, during Obama's presidency state legislators and the Supreme Court severely restricted affirmative action and the hard-fought civil rights protections of the Voting Rights Act of 1965.

Ironically, at the peak of colorblind ideology and the erosion of civil rights protections, TV comedies featuring ethnic and racial minority actors and characters increased. Television scholar Kristen Warner (2015) argues that: "Colorblindness is inherently seductive in a well-intentioned society full of liberal guilt, one that can then avail itself of certain legal discourses, for instance justice is blind and thus objective and fair. These legal discourses are hegemonic and are the foundations of other institutions, especially institutions like television that brand themselves as ideologically socially progressive" (4). The commonsense popular logic of colorblindness presumes a political and cultural climate in which the majority racial group no longer perceives racial difference and therefore cannot legally or socially discriminate based on racial or ethnic identity. In this climate, racially conscious laws, policies, and cultural productions are no longer needed or desirable. The neoliberal political and economic ethos of the twentieth century, which efficiently transferred the U.S.

government's role in education, health, and poverty to the private sphere (churches, community groups, corporations, philanthropic organizations and individuals), could finally be applied to the representation of race or ethnicity and racism on television (Harvey 2005). Obama's election signaled to the public that the governmental, societal, and cultural responsibility in ensuring equality for all could now be deregulated. His election proved that U.S. racism was an individual problem rather than an institutional or federal problem.[3]

African American media studies scholar Catherine Squires (2012) eloquently connects the relationship between neoliberalism and post-racial discourse: "Postracial discourse obfuscates the continued oppressiveness of institutional racism by highlighting individual-level identity choices, thereby dovetailing with neoliberal discourses that place the blame for continuing racial and economic inequalities on individuals who, ostensibly, just made the wrong choices for themselves and/or their families" (545). Indeed, rhetoric studies scholar Darrel Enck-Wanzer (2011) argues that Obama's own presidential language normalized a racial neoliberal ideology. Obama's use of the rhetoric of racial neoliberalism, a speaking strategy that avoided explicit references to race or racism, reinforced the political and popular notion that race was no longer relevant to public policy, political, and cultural life. His speeches, though not his administration's policies, affirmed the long-standing ideological belief in the United States as a colorblind society. As a colorblind society, racism, racial bias, and the reception of racial humor are conceptualized as an individual problem rather than a structural problem of racism embedded in U.S. institutions. In this context, individual audience interpretations of media texts rather than the racial and gender bias of media content production are to blame for problematic TV representations.

Before turning to the characteristics of post-racial TV comedies, I recognize that post-racial discourse in politics, news, and popular culture have a much longer genealogy than the election of President Obama. Conservative scholars and activists have been using color-blindness as an intellectual, political, and cultural strategy since the 1980s to retrench the regulative victories of the Civil Rights era. Writing about the 1980s campaigns against affirmative action and multicultural education policies, Avery Gordon and Christopher Newfield (1996) observed, "The backlash against civil rights achieved its greatest gains not by celebrating white racial consciousness but by officially restricting the relevance of race. It did not defend racism but claimed that racism had passed from the scene" (3). What was "new" about post-racial discourse in the Obama era was its dominance in the popular and political imaginary, produced by mainstream journalism, political pundits, and U.S. TV creators.

Defining Post-Racial TV

First, post-racial TV comedies moved away from the liberal democratic narratives of the 1940s. Sitcoms from the 1940s to 1960s explicitly celebrated ethnic and racial assimilation. The roles played by ethnic and racial minority actors were defined by the characters assimilating into middle-class whiteness and white mainstream culture. For example, shows like *Julia* (1968–71), starring Diahann Carroll, symbolized U.S. political and social progress (Lipsitz 1990) These texts were generally devoid of any ethnic or racial specificity.

Second, post-racial TV sitcoms play with the tokenistic politics of acculturation, cultural authenticity, and social respectability that defined 1980s and 1990s television. TV shows like *The Cosby Show* (1984–92) and *George Lopez* centered on a heteronormative patriarch with storylines focused on the everyday trials and tribulations of acculturated families living the idealized good life of middle-class white America (Gray 1994; Jhally and Lewis 1992). While the comedy in these shows was sometimes specific to African American and Mexican American families, the conflicts and resolutions were universal to white, middle-class, heteronormative culture. The representations in these programs failed to signal to audiences the real-world social context of ethnic and racial minorities at the time (Gray 1994; Markert 2004)

Post-Racial TV, Colorblind, and Multicultural Casting

Instead, post-racial era TV comedies feature ethnic and racial minority in programs that push the boundaries of socially acceptable colorblind humor through the comedy of hipster racism, also known as implied racism. The production practices around colorblindness is most apparent in theater and television casting. Colorblind casting, also referred to as "blindcasting," assumes that skin color or other physical markers of racial or ethnic identity are irrelevant to an actor's ability to perform the role. The 2015 critically acclaimed Broadway show *Hamilton: An American Musical* is perhaps one of the best examples of this practice. The successful musical starred its creator Lin-Manuel Miranda, who is of Puerto Rican descent, and featured a diverse cast of black, Latina/o, African, and Asian American actors playing the predominantly white historical figures surrounding the life of Alexander Hamilton. In television, Shonda Rhimes became the leading proponent of colorblind casting as evidenced by her long-running multicultural ensemble programs *Grey's Anatomy* (2005–Present) and *Scandal* (2012–17). There is an important distinction between Miranda and Rhimes as it regards the analysis of colorblind comedy in this book. While Miranda engages the ethnic and racial specificities of the actors' identities as central to the politically updated characters and storylines of the musical, Rhimes incorporates the diversity of the multicultural ensemble cast in a nonracially conscious manner. In other words, for Rhimes the importance is for audiences to *see* a diversity of faces and not necessarily for the storylines of her shows to tell the ethnically or racially specific stories of those characters (Warner 2015).

Similar to the ways colorblindness operates within the political arena, the assumption of colorblind casting in television is that all actors compete for parts on an equal playing field based on the merits of their skills. However, Warner's work on colorblind TV casting illustrates that the playing field is anything but equal for ethnic and racial minority actors:

> Both colorblindness and casting are founded upon unarticulated assumptions about the irreducibility of physiology—that is, in both cases individuals (casting directors or just ordinary people) assume an equality of opportunity, regardless of physical appearance, thus allowing for a so-called leveling of the playing field where everyone can then perform the same roles without cultural specificity. Practices of colorblindness and casting maintain an idealistic but myopic view of the world based on normative (white) assumptions (2015, 12).

Colorblind casting in television makes visual difference racially insignificant by relying on the development of characters decontextualized from ethnic and racial specificity. The consequence of colorblind casting in TV is that it makes ethnic, racial, and gender difference culturally, socially, and politically irrelevant.

Thus, in post-racial era TV comedies, the storytelling depends on multicultural ensemble casting where the storylines of ethnic and racial actors and characters are sometimes not socially conscious or specifically contextualized by their lived identities or experiences. Television and film scholar Mary Béltran calls the use of this type of casting in cinema "utopic multiculturalism" (2005, 59), a form of multiculturalism where producers use ethnic and racial minority actors as background to create a visual aura of authenticity rather than catalysts for significant storylines foregrounding the experiences of ethnic and racial minorities. Producers of post-racial era TV comedies similarly make the ethnic and racial differences of the actors and characters culturally, socially, and politically visible but usually only as comic background to the white leads and storylines of the show. At its most politically progressive, multicultural ensemble comedies have the potential to be grounded in ethnic or racial social consciousness or what Warner terms "color consciousness." Color-conscious TV programs—for instance, the CW's *Jane the Virgin* or ABC's *Black-ish*—develop characters with ethnic and racial cultural and experiential specificity and thereby more complexity. In its most regressive form, the laughter surrounding ethnic and racial minority characters in post-racial era TV is grounded in what Catherine Squires terms "hipster racism," or implied racism. Post-racial-era TV comedies are often both progressive and regressive at once.

The Post-Racial Comedy of Hipster Racism

Hipster racism refers to the U.S. public's and cultural producers' increased comfort with the use of language and humor that may be coded as racist or sexist. It is referred to by a variety of other terms—modern racism, implied racism, or covert racism. The use of racially loaded language may be explicit—for instance, the increasing use of words like "nigga" for comedic effect. However, in comedies, especially network shows that are more heavily censored by network executives, hipster racism is often implied or inferred. Building on John Fiske's (1996) argument that "[i]nferential racism is the necessary form of racism in a society of white supremacy [or an organization] that proclaims itself non-racist" (37), performance studies scholars Bernadette Calafell (2012) and Tracy Patton (2004) suggest that inferential racism is a central component of the culture of civility grounded in white norms of behavior and social values.

Post-racial-era comedies perpetuate the conditions of cultural civility, whiteness, and inequality through the use of multicultural casting and the ad-libbed and scripted deployment of the comedy of hipster racism. Expanding on Joseph Turow's work on TV's production conventions (1978, 1984, 2000), Warner argues that multicultural representations on contemporary TV are ultimately motivated by the need of television producers and executives to produce and sell happiness to its audiences. Happiness is characterized by the norms and values of whiteness and white civility that demand the erasure of overt signs of social conflict on the screen. Of all TV genres, comedies are perhaps the most amenable to the circulation of hipster racism and colorblind ideology. Writing specifically about Asian American representation, Jane C. H. Park (2014) explains that increases in ethnic and racial minority representations on U.S. sitcoms remain constrained by the continuing "racism, sexism and classism embedded generically within TV narrative content and institutionally within the media entertainment industry" (647). The visual and comedic existence of ethnic and racial minority actors on TV rarely challenges dominant ethnic and racial values and is never portrayed as explicitly threatening to whiteness, white privilege, and the norms of white civility.

Institutional Racism and the Post-Racial TV Production of Hipster Racism

Importantly, as Park (2014) points out, ethnic and racial minority representations in the medium and the comedic genre are partially the result of the lack of diversity within TV production itself. Despite technological innovations and the appearance of representational diversity, the TV production landscape has not changed substantially. Industry reports document the dearth of ethnic and racial minorities within TV programming overall, including Latina/os behind the camera and in the writers room (Hunt, Ramón, and Price, 2014, 2015; Hunt, Ramón, and Tran 2016; Negron-Muntañer, Abbas, Figueroa, and Robson 2014; Smith, Choueiti, and Piper 2014a, 2015, 2016). The ethnic, racial, and gender demographics of people who produce network TV programming and content have remained relatively unchanged since the inception of TV in the 1950s. In stark contrast to the everyday experiences of most U.S. communities, which have seen dramatic demographic shifts, the faces of network executives, producers, and writers remain mostly white and male.

The gender, ethnic, and racial homogeneity of TV executives, content creators, and writers matters because Hollywood is an institution embedded within and informed by the biases of U.S. society, much like any other institution in the United States. As communications historian John Sullivan noted in his work on 1920s and 1930s Hollywood film production, "There is nothing noteworthy about motion picture workers save for the fact that they are the focus of much popular fascination" (2009, 45). In other words, there is nothing exceptional about the identities and lives of the people who create most mainstream entertainment content. Sullivan's observation remains applicable to network TV production today. TV producers are just as likely to hold implicit and explicit ethnic, racial, and gender biases as any other member of the U.S. public. In her critical genealogy of TV production, communications scholar Vicki Mayer (2011) concludes, "New professional organizations, such as Women Make Movies, Women in Film, the National Latino Media Coalition, and the National Asian American Telecommunications Association, dispelled the presumption that the professional TV producer class was not already marked by its whiteness and its masculinity" (13). These organizations act as watchdogs, continually reminding the entertainment industry, scholars, and audiences that TV's creative producers are neither diverse nor colorblind. Creative labor is both the source and cause of inequality in gender, ethnic, and racial representations.

Consequently, a critical component of post-racial era TV comedies is that ethnic, racial, and gender disparities remain in their production. In an era of dramatic demographic change that has born witness to the emergence of Latina/os as the largest minority group in the United States, women and ethnic and racial minorities remain shut out of telling our own stories. In 2016 women make up 4 percent of film directors. Ethnic and racial minorities compose less than 12.5 percent of film directors, and the majority of those directors are African American. Ethnic and racial minority actors are rarely represented by the big five agencies for TV and film and make up less than 5 percent of the big five agencies' acting rosters (Hunt, Ramón, and Tran 2016; Smith, Choueiti, and Piper 2016). From 2010 to 2013 Latina/os did not create any of the top-ten-rated TV and made up only 1.1 percent of TV show producers, 2 percent of writers, and 4.1 percent of directors (Negron-Muntañer, Abbas, Figueroa, and Robson 2014). And as of 2017 no Latina/os currently serve as studio heads, network presidents, CEOs, or owners. Ownership of the means of distribution is even more homogenous than the production of content. Despite post-racial journalistic discourses celebrating the changing face of TV content and TV audiences during the Obama era, the face of TV production and TV content remain predominantly white and male. That means that even when the characters are diverse, the storytellers and those who control the means of production often are not. As I illustrate throughout this book, the lack of diversity in TV production has consequences on the type of storylines, dialogue, characters, and humor surrounding Latina/o characters on contemporary post-racial network sitcoms.

Latina/os and the Comedy of Hipster Racism

It is precisely the post-racial call for colorblindness that makes it safe and funny to represent Latina/os in contemporary TV comedies through hipster racism. Indeed, within the context of the post-racial political environment, Latina/os became the key object and subject of racial humor through the deployment of "hipster racism" or "equal-opportunity offending" (Esposito 2009; Squires 2014). Post-racial-era sitcoms produce hipster racism through plot, narrative, and dialogue that create a scripted space of comedic ambiguity where gender, race, and ethnicity are written into the show in ways not previously socially permissible on network TV without risking political backlash from audiences or advertisers.

In using the terms "post-racial TV" and "hipster racism," I am not suggesting that race, ethnicity, gender, and sexuality are ignored in these sitcoms, because they are not. Instead I build on the work of critical race scholar Ashley Doane, who argues "for a more nuanced view of colorblind racial ideology, one that moves beyond a simple focus on the denial of racism and instead emphasizes the ability to hold simultaneous—and contradictory—positions—for example, that racial inequality and white privilege persist, but that racism is not widespread" (2014, 17). The narratives of post-racial sitcoms indeed *use* sexism, homophobia, racism, and xenophobia alongside the multicultural representation of racial, ethnic, gender, and sexual difference as a strategy to produce humor. As Doane proposes, "In a 'colorblind' world, race is most often (but not always) defined as the characteristic of individuals in a world where racism is no longer a major factor and race plays no meaningful role in the distribution of resources" (2014, 17). The underlying assumption made by network executives and show creators appears to be that audiences are living in a moment when the popular and commonsense belief is that representations of ethnic, racial, and gender differences no longer carry social or political consequences and are therefore fair comedic game.

Hipster racism in post-racial comedies is then produced through conscious, unconscious, and implied verbal and nonverbal putdowns as well as slapstick and physical comedy that make fun of race, ethnic, gender, and sexual difference. The humor depends on audiences' own comfort and relationship to racism, sexism, homophobia, and xenophobia. And it relies on more complicated plots, ambiguously interpreted dialogue, and complex character relationships than sitcoms in the past. The deployment of hipster racism as a generic device in contemporary sitcoms serves two institutional purposes. First, it allows network executives to attract the economic capital of white audiences/consumers while safely reaching out to ethnic and racial minority audiences/consumers. Second, it creates the marketable appearance that TV network executives are responsive to demands by activists for diversity in programming and production.

In *Modern Family*, like the other comedies produced from 2007 to 2016, the scripted production of hipster racism is possible, as sitcom scholar Brett Mills (2009) suggests, because of generic innovation. Comedies during this time period have undergone major production and technological changes to the genre. One of the primary transformations in contemporary TV comedies is the removal of the laugh track. The laugh track in sitcoms played a socially significant role as it cued audiences into who and what was being laughed at and whether it was socially appropriate to laugh at the joke: "[A sitcom] . . . laugh track doesn't just suggest that something is funny; it suggests something is obviously clearly, unarguably, un-problematically funny, and that such responses are collectively defined and experienced" (Mills 2009, 81). The laugh track provides for the "venting of nervous energy" by assuming a tacit social agreement between the beliefs and values of the audiences and producers, especially regarding socially complex or controversial issues (Mills 2009, 81).

Without the laugh track, comedic writing depends on the subtext rather than text. Thus, the production of laughter through hipster racism relies instead on the *intercultural* relationships between the show's multicultural ensemble cast and the *intertextual* references to ethnicity and race in an everyday context. Intertextuality within a TV show is used by TV writers to reference the social world outside and produce a sense of realism. Intertextual references may be other cultural texts (e.g., TV shows, songs, films) or people, events, experiences, language, or popular fads in the world outside the screen. The use of intertextuality in sitcoms also provides an opportunity to track changes within TV's symbolic landscape as a social institution (Turow 2000). Intertextuality has become a significant element of modern TV comedies. For instance, in his analysis of the British version of *The Office*, Mills (2009) observed the humor relied less on the generic conventions of sitcoms (slapstick, laugh track, routine comedic set-ups) and more on audiences' personal familiarity with the narratives and contemporary issues depicted on the show. In the context of the U.S. version of *The Office*, the character of Michael (Steve Carell) is funny because audiences themselves are already familiar with the social conventions regarding racism, sexism, and homophobia that he routinely breaks. Carell's performance of a well-meaning but socially inappropriate boss becomes an intertextual reference point for the show's audiences as his character may remind them of family members, office workmates, or friends. Said another way, the comedic scripting of hipster racism and the popularity of socially inappropriate characters in comedies as well as the greenlighting of these shows by network executives tells us something about the broader social and political context in which these innovations and decisions are made. In sum, the emergence of hipster racism on comedic TV speaks to the social context as it is shaped by the dominance of colorblind ideology and the dynamics of power in media institutions.

Latina/os and Hipster Racism on Post-Racial TV

The seminal work of Charles Ramirez-Berg (2000) on Latina/os in film and Mary Béltran (2008) on Latina/os in film and television document the narratives, stereotypes, and archetypes that have historically defined ethnic and racial visibility for Latina/os and Latin Americans in Hollywood. Cinematic and television texts that include Latina/o characters generally center on white male protagonists who are cast as moral, resourceful, brave, intelligent, and overall racially superior to the secondary Latina/o archetypes. Latina/o characters, however, are often characterized in stereotypical and mostly binary ways as the Latin lover or harlot, the dark lady or bandito, the female clown or male buffoon, and the señorita. The Latin lover and harlot are archetypes depicting Latin American–descendent characters as more emotional, romantic, and sexual than white characters. The dark lady and bandito archetypes emphasize the duplicitous or untrustworthy nature of the characters, and the female clown, also known as the spitfire, and male buffoon are comedic archetypes that parody Latin American cultures. All the types are depicted as more sexual than their white counterparts except for the señorita archetype, who is often a character defined by her religious virtue and conservative sexual morality. These observations continue to hold true on TV. Two of the most memorable Latina characters on post-2009 TV are Gloria Pritchett (Sofía Vergara), a version of the Latin spitfire, and Jane Villanueva (Gina Rodriguez), a type of señorita.

Research on contemporary Latina/os in film and TV point to an overwhelming tendency toward representing Latina/os as cultural threats and eternal foreigners in the United States (Amaya 2013; Béltran 2010; Del Rio 2006; Molina-Guzmán 2010; Valdivia 2010). Additionally, the persistent invisibility and erasure of differences across ethnic-specific groups is the norm in the mainstream media. When Latina/os are depicted, those media representations are mostly based on gender, sexuality, race, ethnicity, and citizenship stereotypes about Latina/os that reinforce the dominant regime of representation on TV (Amaya 2013; Del Rio 2006; Molina-Guzmán 2010). Interestingly, shows like *Modern Family* and *Superstore* also illustrate how colorblind comedy sometimes works against the regime of representation by "winking" with Latina/o audiences through the use of ambiguous humor that subtly calls attention to whiteness and white privilege. Those same characters, narratives, and humor produce the more conservative comedy of hipster racism, demonstrating the ways these TV texts culturally work in simultaneously progressive and regressive ways.

Latina/o Visibility in Post-Racial-Era Media

The hypervisibility of a few actors such as Vergara, Jennifer Lopez, and Michael Peña makes it appear to audiences that Latina/os are everywhere in the entertainment media, yet the reality, as pointed to earlier, is that Latina/os remain relatively invisible in film and TV. In the seven hundred top-grossing Hollywood films released from 2007 to 2016 (Smith, Choueiti, and Piper 2017), 70.8 percent of speaking roles in those movies went to white characters, 13.6 percent to African Americans, 5.7 percent to Asians, and only 3.1 percent to Latina/os. While the number of African American and Asian characters increased from 2014, the percentage of Latina/o characters declined. Men outnumber women in all groups, and both Latina and Latino characters remain more likely to be depicted in highly sexual ways than any other racial or ethnic group. Indeed, the report found that women, girls, Latinas, and Latinos were more likely to be shown either partially or fully naked or in revealing clothing.

Turning to TV, the terrain is not much more encouraging as 11.4 percent of lead characters in the 2016 season were ethnic and racial minorities, an improvement from 8.1 percent of lead characters in 2016 (Hunt, Ramón, and Tran 2017). In the 2015 TV season, Latina/o characters made up 5.1 percent of speaking roles (Smith, Choueiti, and Piper 2016). In supporting film and TV roles portrayed by Latina/os, most of the characters were criminals, law enforcers, or cheap labor; Latinas played 67 percent of maid roles on TV (Negron-Muntañer, Abbas, Figueroa, and Robson 2014). Ethnic and racial minority representation across TV platforms (broadcast, cable, streaming) illustrates a similar pattern of invisibility, with streaming TV being the

least diverse (Smith, Choueiti, and Piper 2016). The hypersexualiza-
tion of Latina/o characters in film and television remains a dominant
narrative convention. Indeed, Latina characters are the most likely of
all ethnic and racial groups to be depicted in sexualized attire, partially nude, or as the object of heterosexual sexual attraction (Smith,
Choueiti, and Piper 2016). Latina/os are the largest ethnic and racial
minority group in the United States, but Latina/o characters are
almost invisible, and when they are visible it is in mostly stereotyped
ways.

Casting Latina/os on Post-Racial Sitcoms

Some of the most critically acclaimed and highly rated TV comedy
shows from 2007 to 2016 either featured secondary cast members
or lead actors of color. These post-racial era programs succeeded
by targeting younger and wealthier predominantly white audiences
who made up the large share of viewers making more than $100,000
per year, one of the most coveted demographics for TV advertisers
(Cantor 2014; Kissel 2013). Chapter 2 examines how post-racial era
comedies, such as *Modern Family*, transformed representations of
Latina/o identity while simultaneously producing culturally familiar
and safe conventions for ethnic and queer characters. The audience's
acceptance of colorblind humor and the comedy of hipster racism
in programs like *Modern Family* depend on multicultural ensemble
casting and strategically comic roles played by Latina/o actors, especially Latinas, in post-racial era programs.

So, what does casting the Latina/o look mean in television? In
Latinos Inc: The Marketing and Making of a People (2001), cultural
anthropologist Arlene Dávila defines the "Latin look" as a set of
physical and cultural characteristics used to cast commercial actors
and models in Hispanic media. The Latin look is defined as an actor
who appears exotic but is racially ambiguous, dark haired (long
haired if a woman), and a fluent Spanish speaker or a fluent English
speaker with a slight Spanish accent. In Hispanic advertising and
marketing, the models or actors should portray roles that are family oriented, heterosexual, emotionally passionate, and ideologically conservative. English-language television producers employ
the Latin look to add stereotypic visual diversity. For instance, as

is common knowledge, Sofía Vergara dyed her hair from blond to black to successfully access the U.S. English-language media market (Molina-Guzmán 2014). Interestingly, most likely due to her commercial U.S. success, Vergara returned to her natural hair color in later seasons of *Modern Family*.

Casting Latina/os on primetime sitcoms then depends on the inclusion of actors and characters who can perform the Latin look in expected and predictable ways, such as Gloria in *Modern Family*. Other network comedies such as *The Office* and *Parks and Recreation*, however, have worked against type in the casting of Latina/o characters by hiring actors who do not easily conform to the Latin look or stereotypic performance of Latina/o characters. Chapter 3 looks at comedies such as these that potentially draw audiences' attention to their own expectations and familiarity with Latino stereotypes in the mainstream media. For example, Aubrey Plaza, who plays April on *Parks and Recreation*, is Puerto Rican and has the Latin look, but she performs against the TV stereotype of Latinas in every other way on the show. Chapter 1 focuses on the role Afro-Latina/os play in decentering audiences' expectations in colorblind comedies, such as Judy Reyes (Carla in *Scrubs*), who performs an Afro-Dominican nurse, and Oscar Nuñez (Oscar in *The Office*), who performs a gay, politically conservative Afro-Mexican accountant.

To fully understand the role of Latina/o characters in colorblind comedy, we must first situate the politics of casting Latina/os on TV. In U.S. television production Latina/o actors are typecast and Latina/o characters are stereotyped in particular ways (Béltran 2009; Noriega 2000). Typecasting refers to hiring actors for the same type of parts or roles on the basis of physical appearance, cultivated off-air personality, or previous roles. Stereotyping involves the repeated use of simplified positive or negative characteristics generalized to a particular social group to develop characters (Ramirez-Berg 2000; Wojcik 2003). Economic pressures in television often lead to copying formulas for casting, characters, and genres that are proven successes in terms of audience ratings, advertising revenue, and narrative conventions around ethnicity and race (Gitlin 2000; Noriega 2000). The copycat effect, for instance, led to the proliferation of reality TV programming at the turn of the millennium and the rise of mockumentary sitcoms from 2007 to 2014.

TV program development, which is much more constrained than film in terms of scheduling and content regulation, makes most TV writers dependent on stock character stereotypes and archetypes inherited from popular film texts. Using stock characters allows TV producers to communicate information quickly to audiences (Pieracinni and Alligood 2005). The problem for TV writers is when stock characters and character archetypes become associated with racial stereotypes, such as the Latina spitfire: "When archetypes take on stereotypical tones, the storyworld becomes invaded by prejudicial and demeaning images" (Gray 2008, 106). In post-racial era sitcoms, the humor surrounding Latina/o characters either revolves around the actors playing to (Vergara as Gloria) or, more interestingly, against typecasting and stereotyped archetypes (Nuñez as Oscar).

The contemporary effectiveness of Latina/o typecasting and stereotyping in post-racial TV is complicated. In 1980 the U.S. Census's classification of "Latinos" as an ethnic rather than racial category reinforced mainstream news and popular constructions of Latina/os as a pan-ethnic group defined by racial ambiguity and therefore no race in particular (Oboler 1995; Rodriguez 2000). Journalists in mainstream media industry publications such as *Variety* and *Ad Age* picked up and recirculated the Census discourse about Latina/os' pan-ethnic identity and racial ambiguity in the 1990s through narratives such as the "browning of America." By highlighting "brown" as a racial category, the news coverage highlighted the growing demographic importance of Latina/o audiences and the ability of multiracial or racially ambiguous Latina/o actors to draw in diverse and larger global audiences (Molina-Guzmán and Valdivia 2004; Silva 2016). One of the leading examples used by journalists as evidence of the browning of popular culture was the casting of Nuyorican (New York–born Puerto Rican) Jennifer Lopez to play the iconic role of *Selena* (1997). Director Gregory Nava believed young girls and women across ethnic and racial categories inside and outside of the United States would relate to Lopez and the famous Tejana (Texan-born U.S. Mexican) singer she portrayed (Béltran 2009; Molina-Guzmán 2010; Paredez 2010). Similarly, mixed-race Mexican American Jessica Alba was cast in the lead role of the racially and ethnically ambiguous Max in the television show *Dark Angel* (2000–2002) because showrunner James Cameron thought her exotic "transgenetic" appearance fit the character best (Béltran and Fojas 2008; Kloer 2003; Molina-Guzmán 2013). Cameron believed Alba's lack of definable racial identity was ambiguous enough to be read as any identity, and for him, this ambiguity was central to the character and the narrative. Thus, the casting of most Latina/o actors on post-racial era TV programming reaffirmed the popular notion that U.S. Latina/os are racially ambiguous and outside of the U.S. black-white racial binary.

Consequently, finding actors to play Latina/o characters generally means hiring people that have the Latin look, may be read by audiences as ambiguously brown (i.e., not black), and cannot be categorized within any particular ethnicity or race. Along with the performance of an ambiguous racial identity, actors cast to play Latina/o roles generally have dark hair and dark eyes as well as voluptuous feminine bodies or muscular masculine bodies, among other physical characteristics. Dávila (2008) actually notes that over the past fifteen years, casting by both English- and Spanish-language media has overwhelmingly skewed toward Latina/o models and actors like Sofía Vergara who can perform both Latina identity and whiteness.

Actors who have the Latin look and can perform the Latina/o type are most often cast in the stereotypical role of the Latina/o exotic, a role that adds a semblance of diversity to a mostly white or multiracial ensemble TV show. In other words, casting Latina/os on primetime TV relies on the convergence of ethnic and racial typecasting and ethnic stereotypes and archetypes. It is a regime of representation where Latina/o characters are few and those that do appear entertain through a flattening of the diversity of Latina/o identities and experiences across gender, sexuality, race, ethnicity, and citizenship (Del Rio 2006). Latina/o actors on urban sitcoms such as *Brooklyn Nine-Nine* are sometimes used to add visual and ethnic authenticity. In other post-racial era comedies, Latina/o actors are part of a multicultural ensemble cast where they are the likely, socially safe recipients of the comedy of hipster racism. Most U.S. TV representations of Latina/o identity, such as that of Gloria on *Modern Family*, rely on the production of familiar ethnic characteristics that stereotypically communicate national origin through the use of language, dress, or music, such as the use of Spanish, dance, or salsa music.

Spinning Latina/o Audiences and Television Visibility

The relative invisibility of Latina/o TV characters in the historical context of Latina/o demographic growth creates an interesting cultural paradox. According to the Pew Research Center (2015), Latina/os in 2015 made up 17.4 percent of the U.S. population. Although the Asian American population grew at a faster rate, Latina/os emerged as the largest ethnic and racial minority group in 2015. As a result of Latina/o demographic growth, California, Texas, and New Mexico became majority-minority states. Some demographers predict that by 2044 the United States will be a majority-minority nation (Pew Research Center 2015). Latina/o population growth combined with increased economic power has attracted the interest of mainstream TV producers and the advertisers and subscription services sustaining that TV content. However, Latina/o market power has not fully translated to significant or proportional mainstream cultural visibility, a paradox that has been termed as the "Latino media gap" (Negron-Muntañer, Abbas, Figueroa, and Robson 2014). Put another way, even though the U.S. Latina/o population has grown since the 1950s, the media presence of Latina/os actually shrank during that same time period.

In 2014, the Nielsen Company estimated the purchasing power of Latina/os at $1.4 trillion (Aranda-Mori 2014). It also confirmed that while bilingual homes watch English- and Spanish-language TV in about equal proportions, in English-dominant households only 3 percent of viewers watched TV in Spanish (Pardo and Dreas 2011). Latina/o language use matters in the context of English-language television because, demographically, the population of non-U.S.-born, Spanish-dominant Latina/os declined in 2016, making the majority of U.S. Latina/os U.S. born as well as English-dominant or English-proficient speakers. English-dominant or English-proficient speakers are likely to consume their media in English and prefer TV programming that mirrors U.S. white viewership trends (Medialife 2015; Pieracinni and Alligood 2005). In 2016, U.S.-born Latinos outnumbered foreign-born immigrants by nearly two-to-one—thirty-five million to nineteen million. Additionally, U.S.-born Latina/os made up 65 percent of the nation's Latina/o population and were much younger with a median age of nineteen years compared to the median age of forty years among immigrant Latina/os (Patten 2016). The most desirable demographic for advertisers is the eighteen-to-thirty-nine-year-old demographic, and eighteen-to-thirty-nine-year-old Latina/o and African American audiences watch more TV, both digital and legacy, than any other demographic group (Nielsen Company 2014).

One might assume that these numbers would result in making Latina/o audiences matter to advertisers, marketers, and media content creators. But the numbers have not translated to greater media visibility or political representation. Dávila (2008) labels the emphasis on the demographic and economic information mentioned in the previous paragraph by Latina/o or Hispanic marketers, media producers, and politicians as "Latino spin." The cultural and political spinning of Latina/os as a socially respectable, normative, powerful, and profitable market from 2000 to 2010 actually contributes to the group's continued cultural and political invisibility. That is, Latino spin depends on the ethnic and racial whitewashing and middle-class homogenization of Latina/o identity in everything from advertising to TV and film. Spinning Latina/os as a desirable economic class and part of the cultural and political mainstream constructs Latina/os as a socially safe population to court as voters, consumers, and audiences. It also makes Latina/os culturally safe to represent in mainstream entertainment media but only through depictions that reinforce pan-ethnic white normativity. Dávila's observation underlies the core questions of this book: How do political, market, and media industry forces shape the depictions of the few Latina/o actors and characters on TV? And what are the cultural consequences of that visibility in the U.S. cultural, political, and economic landscape of the post-racial era?

Book Outline

The sitcoms discussed in this book incorporate Latina/o identity in ways that reinforce the traditional conservative ideology of the genre. At the same time, the programs' production strategies also create a space for Latina/o and other ethnic and racial minority audiences. The sitcoms are able to achieve both strategies through the following characteristics:

- Colorblind or multicultural ensemble casting
- Colorblind humor
- Comedy of hipster racism

These characteristics allow the programs to appeal to audiences in two ways. First, the comedy speaks to non-Latino audiences in ways that are ethnically and racially progressive and regressive. Second, the comedic ambiguity incorporates ethnic and racial minority audiences through multicultural casting and the comic ambiguity introduced through hipster racism. Colorblind humor is not a particularly new strategy on U.S. television programs aired from 2007 to 2016. It is, however, a strategy that takes on a particular political significance during the Obama presidency. During the historically unprecedented presidency of the first mixed-race African American man, Latinos emerged as the largest ethnic and racial minority group and a politically and socially embattled demographic class. Both U.S. Latina/os and Obama faced increased ethnic and racial hostility during the same time period.

Chapter 1, "*Scrubs*(ing) the Beginnings of Post-Racial TV," focuses on the early years of post-racial TV by tracing the genealogy of Latina/o actors. The analysis begins with the influence of the September 11th terrorist attacks on political and televisual culture. In particular, *Scrubs* is employed as a case study for examining the effective practice of multicultural ensemble casting and socially conscious writing during the early 2000s. Together, the casting of *Scrubs* and the use of socially conscious humor in addition to Reyes's performance of the antiexotic Latina illuminate the possibilities for ethnic and racial inclusion in post-racial era programming. Particular attention is paid to Reyes's straight comedic character and the role she plays in highlighting whiteness and white privilege. The key conventions of post-racial era comedies are defined and developed through the analysis of *Scrubs*.

In chapter 2, "Hipster Racism Comes to Colorblind TV," *The Office* and *Modern Family* are engaged as exemplary case studies of the comedy of hipster racism as a central convention in post-racial era comedies. The programs are contextualized within the historical periods in which they first aired. Foregrounding the use of multicultural casting and colorblind humor, the concept of hipster racism is developed by discussing the Latina/o characters in relation to a program's white leads. Hipster racism is defined as the use of explicit or implicit xenophobic, racist, sexist, or homophobic writing and character development. The production of hipster racism in the postracial TV era is linked to the diversity, or lack thereof, of the writers room. Chapter 2 documents the relationship between the diversity of the production team and the creation of colorblind humor and hipster racism regarding ethnicity and race as well as character development for actors of color.

Revisiting the progressive possibilities of post-racial era TV, chapter 3, "Reading against the Post-Racial TV Latina," returns to the antiexotic Latina and colorblind ideology of chapter 1 to make sense of comedies produced and aired after 2008. The analysis reflects on the potential cracks or moments of disjuncture in post-racial era sitcoms grounded in colorblind ideology by thinking through the transformative possibilities of the comedic performances by Vergara (*Modern Family*) and Plaza (*Parks and Recreation*). Chapter 3 reengages the post-racial era antiexotic Latina of chapter 1 to analyze Plaza's performance and rereads Vergara's more gender and racially normative performance of the Latina spitfire. The chapter first situates Plaza's performance of whiteness and Latinidad as an antiexotic, straight comedic character who disrupts stereotypes and white norms of respectability and privilege. Vergara's more normative performance of gender and Latinidad is reread as an exotic, straight comedic character who also critiques whiteness and white privilege. Focusing on the producers' development of Vergara's character as a complex Latina mother and an undocumented Colombian immigrant, my reading frustrates the stereotypic development of Latina TV visibility.

The book's conclusion, "Post-Racial Past and Colorblind Futures on TV" explores the political and cultural critique of post-racial discourse and TV producers' creative move away from the comedy of hipster racism. Studying post-2014 colorblind programs like *Jane the Virgin* and *Superstore*, I document TV producers' return to the ideologically less complicated feel-good ethos of "basic" comedic programming. Specifically, the narratives and character development are analyzed as the colorblind deployment of acculturation by the writers of these shows. Contextualizing the post-2014 TV landscape within

U.S. anti-immigrant and anti-black discourses as well as the Trump campaign and election, I illustrate the high cultural stakes embedded in TV comedy as well as the limits of representations of ethnic and racial difference.

Modern Family is used as a significant cultural referent throughout the book because the program makes hypervisible the cultural labor of Latino actors and characters on popular U.S. sitcoms. In doing so, this book calls into question the conservative values of meritocracy reinforced in TV comedies that ultimately maintain whiteness and heterosexuality as the representational norm. Latina/o gains in primetime TV comedies are evidence of social and political postracial progress even as the market-driven motives for their inclusion are erased. Drawing attention to the strategic casting of Latina/o TV visibility illustrates the continuing dominance of post-racial discourse, a discourse that obscures the structural inequality and disenfranchisement of Latinos, African Americans, and other ethnic and racial minority groups in the United States.

Chapter 1

SCRUBS(ING) THE BEGINNINGS OF POST-RACIAL TV

CARLA: *Word does get around, Ms. "Out For Herself," so you can dump on everyone here if you want; but you will not hurt me.*

EXCERPT FROM *SCRUBS*'S "MY FIRST DAY"

It is not accidental that incremental increases in Latina/o visibility coincide with the emergence of post-racial comedy. *George Lopez* (2002–7), which had a short on-air run, proved that Latina/os could be funny and that television audiences would tune in to watch a Latino actor as a comedic lead on a family sitcom. The show never broke into the top twenty programs in the Nielsen ratings and was eventually canceled by ABC after five seasons. In the mid-2000s, television—comedies in particular—ran into the headwinds of industry as well as political and social changes. Two major events occurred that would change the television landscape forever: the low production costs and high popularity of the reality TV genre and the September 11th terrorist attack in New York City (Gray 2008).

After the September 11th attacks, a desire for smart comfort TV fueled speculations that sitcoms would experience a comeback of sorts for a genre that most believed was in cultural decline (Carter 2001). That fall most TV executives decided to stick with the premiere of sitcoms such as *Scrubs*, which was initially slated to air for the first time on the week of the attacks. The anxiety-ridden realities facing U.S. audiences called for more soothing, familiar, and escapist fare. TV shows like *Survivor* (2000–Present), fantasy dramas such as *Lost* (2004–10), and over-the-top dramedies such as *Desperate Housewives* (2004–12) ruled the airwaves. During this period, family sitcoms in particular faced major changes. The producers of family sitcoms, like *Malcolm in the Middle* (2000–2006), moved television comedies and their families into more visually and socially realistic settings while simultaneously inhabiting them with more absurd characters and storylines. It was a return of sorts to the sitcoms of the past that often centered on the universal everyday concerns of white, heteronormative, middle-class families.

Television comedies such as *Scrubs* uniquely straddled this changing social and television environment by meeting the moment's increasing demand for realistic comedy with an absurd escapist tone created through the use of running gags, dream sequences, and even a musical. It took showrunner Bill Lawrence two years to find a home for the innovative single-camera workplace sitcom, filmed in a decommissioned North Hollywood hospital. According to Lawrence, network executives were concerned about both the cost of filming a sitcom in a live set instead of taping it in a studio and the blending of absurd comedy with highly emotional drama (Turow 2000). Executives were especially wary about the depiction of death in a sitcom, as death is generally a taboo subject in TV comedies. *Scrubs'* mixture of drama and familiar sitcom conventions like slapstick humor, physical comedy, and recurring jokes softened the realistic life-and-death decisions being made by the medical characters. The show's first two episodes were filmed as the events of September 11th unfolded in the news. The visceral emotional tone of the show in the context of national angst struck a compelling note with the program's young and loyal audience.[1]

Eventually, the premise drew the interest of network executives at NBC and television critics who hailed the multicultural ensemble cast of the show. As discussed in the introduction, ethnic and racial demographic trends at the turn of the millennium drew the attention of cultural activists, TV executives, and industry trade journals. The positive critical reception of *Scrubs* pointed to the effectiveness of multicultural ensemble casting. Comedic shows with multicultural casts became a hallmark characteristic of post-racial TV. Programs like *Scrubs* also signaled the possibilities for socially conscious comedy explicitly grounded in contemporary identity politics, an uncommon type of writing about ethnicity, race, and sexuality that would not appear again until the emergence of original streaming content like Netflix's *One Day at a Time* (2017–Present) and *Dear White People* (2017–Present). Unpacking the success of post-racial era comedies such as *Modern Family* requires an understanding of how shows like

Scrubs and *The Office* (chapter 2) changed the conventions for TV representations of ethnicity, race, and Latina/os.

Producing Multicultural Ensemble Sitcoms: Breaking the Fourth Wall

The October 2001 premiere of *Scrubs* marked a new era in network sitcom programming. Beginning in the 1970s, sitcoms became approximately twenty-two minutes in length, filmed on a theater-style proscenium stage using three cameras, performed by a recurring cast of characters before a live or taped studio audience, and enhanced by a laugh track to signal what was funny and when it was appropriate to laugh (Mills 2009; Savorelli 2010). The stage was usually broken up into separate, mechanically rotating rooms (living room, kitchen, office, etc.) with three walls, and the same rooms were generally used every episode (Mills 2009). The invisible wall between the actors and the audience is referred to as the fourth wall. More important, the narratives used a traditional setup/conflict/happy-resolution structure that featured stock, archetypical, and stereotypical characters along with other comedic conventions for traditional sitcoms, such as the slapstick comedy derived from theater and radio serials (Mills 2009). *Scrubs* contributed to the transformation of sitcom conventions in interesting ways (Savorelli 2010). The sitcom marked a return to using a single 16mm film camera. As mentioned earlier, it was also the first to be filmed outside of a production studio and to successfully feature a multicultural ensemble comedic cast. Lastly, it was one of the few sitcoms in U.S. TV history to blend drama, comedy, and filmic special effects.[2] The combination of these innovations created a unique opportunity for representing gender, ethnicity, race, and Latina/o characters in the wake of September 11th and the deep fear and resentment of ethnic and racial minorities it produced.

By moving out of the traditional sound stage, the producers allowed the camera to play with space and time, thereby making the camera a central part of the narrative (Savorelli 2010). Using a single camera in a live set rather than a studio stage increased the level of visual realism. The use of film in *Scrubs* also allowed for the incorporation of special sound and visual effects as well as the incorporation of surrealistic narrative elements most often found in feature films, such as dream sequences and musical montages. *The Office* copied the single-camera format to produce the documentary effect since copied by other post-racial TV comedies. These types of programs invite the camera to break the fourth wall between writer and performer and the audience, making audiences conscious of their role in making sense of the narrative. As an omnipresent and omniscient presence, the audience as cameraperson and documentarian becomes privy to the internal emotions, private conflicts, and the "unseen" actions and motivations of the characters on the program. The camera and, by extension, the audience become part of the narrative.

Socially Conscious Writing

Although *Scrubs*—similar to a majority of sitcoms—was created by a white man and starred a white male actor, the writing for the multi-racial ensemble cast presented a radical departure from the all-white ensemble casts and writing staffs of its highly rated contemporaries such as *Friends* (1994–2004), *Two and a Half Men* (2003–15), and *Everybody Loves Raymond* (1996–2005). The diversity of the writers room was also important to understanding the representation of ethnic and racial difference on *Scrubs*.[3] In a marked departure from other legacy and digital television programs, the actors and writers of color played substantial roles in developing the characters, producing the narratives, and the ethnic and racial humor of the show (Savorelli 2010).

NBC Studios' Ted Harbert handpicked Lawrence (*Scrubs*) to create what would become *Scrubs*. Both men had worked together on the show *Spin City* (1992–2002). Lawrence brought on his close friend and longtime creative collaborator Randall Winston, an openly gay African American producer and writer (Adalian 2001a, 62). Winston also worked with Lawrence as an executive producer for *Spin City* and became a co-executive producer for *Scrubs*. From the show's inception, Lawrence saw the interracial male friendship between J.D. (Zack Braff) and Turk (Donald Faison) as a primary narrative theme in the show. And he envisioned Winston as the central writer for the relationship between the male characters. Indeed, the unabashedly homosocial and often outright queer nature of the characters' male friendship produced some of the funniest recurring lines and moments in the show (Halterman 2014). Along with Winston, *Scrubs'* writers room also included two women, a rarity in the mostly white male world of television sitcoms.[4] The loss of the proscenium stage and the laugh track, the increased diversity in the writers room, and the multicultural ensemble cast of *Scrubs* resulted in the creation of socially conscious humor and comedy. Through Carla Espinosa (Judy Reyes), the primary Latina character on the show, the writing team set up one of the more interesting conventions regarding representations of ethnicity, race, and gender in the post-racial era TV comedy: the antiexotic comedic straight "man." For the producers, the Afro-Latina character was central to achieving the color consciousness of the program.

Scrubs and the Antiexotic Latina

From its screening at the 2001 first looks in New York, *Scrubs* was described as "fitting the mold of smart, upscale sitcoms such as 'Friends' and 'Frasier'" (Freeman 2001).[5] Indeed, Lawrence began his career as a staff writer on *Friends*, and *Scrubs* was pitched as an updated version of *Friends* in a hospital setting. The writers for *Scrubs* targeted its comedy at an affluent, educated, and white audience. The show averaged about 6.4 million viewers and never broke into the top ten in the Nielsen ratings, but the affluent "nerdy cultish fanbase" of the show online kept the networks interested for nine years (Heisler 2009).

Along with its "upscale audience profile," the show presented TV executives with a unique opportunity to market its multicultural casting and demonstrate the network's commitment to diversity. This element of the pitch was picked up by trade journalists: "Another potential help for 'Scrubs' in the ratings race: The almost effortless diversity of the show's cast, which includes black and Latina actors in key roles" (Adalian 2001b, A18). Executive producer Lawrence openly talked about the show's diversity and how the interracial homosocial friendship was a central narrative theme: "'One of the things I've always wanted to do in a TV show is have a black guy and a white guy be best friends, and not have that be the story,' Lawrence says" (Adalian 2001b, A18). In a twist on socially conscious comedy but exemplary of post-racial colorblind writing, Lawrence wanted the ethnic and racial specificities of the characters to be an element of the narrative without the storylines and character development being motivated by race, racial difference, or racial inequality.

Afro-Latina/o Actors as Antiexotic Characters

Sometimes identified as racially black because of skin color and physiognomy and also classified as Latina/o because of ethnic origin, Afro-Latina/o actors negotiate a typecasting culture that privileges whiteness and stereotypical assumptions about body and physical appearance bound in the "Latin look." In her book on blackness and Puerto Rican television, communications historian Yeidy Rivero (2005) documents the often-denigrating comedic use of black racial identity in English- and Spanish-language sitcoms. If Latina/o typecasting in Hollywood usually takes the form of voluptuous olive-skinned Latinas and muscular well tanned Latinos, then casting Reyes as Carla disrupts the regime of Latina/o representation discussed in the introduction. Carla's character and Reyes's comedic performance produced a new Latina/o type: the antiexotic Latina.

Antiexotic Latina/o characters challenge TV producers' use of stock characters and ethnic and racial sitcom stereotypes. By casting against type, producers develop Latina/o characters who do not fit with audiences' visual and narrative expectations for the cultural reproduction of whiteness and hypersexualized Latina/o bodies. Antiexotic Latina/o characters and the actors who portray them create a type of cognitive dissonance for audiences as a result of their stereotypic assumptions about Latina/os not cohering with the visual world of television. Cast as a highly skilled and respected nurse on *Scrubs*, Reyes performed the role of the post-racial antiexotic comedic straight man. The antiexotic straight man is a role that draws attention to ethnic, racial, and gender biases of the other characters through the use of humor but does not directly question the whiteness of the program's characters and overall narrative. *Scrubs'* writers engaged the antiexotic straight-man role instead of hipster racism to produce the ethnic and racial humor of the show.

From its creation, Lawrence clearly situates the character's Latina ethnicity as central to the role. In the script for the pilot, Carla is described as "Hispanic, thirtyish, painfully frank, and manages to be motherly and sexy at the same time" (Lawrence 2001, 7). As such, the casting of Reyes is not an example of colorblind casting. It is instead color-conscious casting as the ethnic identity of the character is central to the role. In *Scrubs*, the writers merged two of the main media tropes for performing Latina femininity (Latina motherhood and Latina hypersexuality) to create the Carla character. Using a Stuart Hall–like reversal of stereotypes, Lawrence inverted both the motherhood and hypersexuality tropes through the development of a strong and complex Latina character not predominantly defined by her gender, ethnicity, or race (Hall 1997). Reyes was the only actor cast by the producers who did not have to go through the entire casting process. *Scrubs*' producers auditioned Reyes by tape and flew her in for a single screen test in front of network executives before offering her the role. The producers identified and actively recruited her for the role of Carla. None of the other ensemble actors were exempt from the full casting process, indicating that Lawrence specifically wanted the U.S.-born Dominican actor Reyes for that role.

Scrubs also provided Reyes with a significant acting opportunity to work against the Latina typecasting and stereotyping culture that, up to that point, had defined her career on television: "I mean, even early in my career when I first started I would be asked to do a Rosie Perez prototype or, you know, do a heavy accent or ramble off in Spanish for people who don't speak Spanish. It turned out to be just for, you know, the amusement of non-Latinos" (Sheridan 2006). A look at Reyes's IMDB (n.d.) page documents her performances in minor nonrecurring and stereotypic television roles. In the first minor role listed on the page, she played a Catholic nun on *Law and Order* ("Sisters of Mercy" 1992); in one of her latest starring roles, she played a smart, no-nonsense Latina maid (*Devious Maids* 2013–16).

In contrast to the majority of TV roles she has played, Reyes's performance on *Scrubs* creates a space to contest stereotypic messages about women, Latinas, Dominicans, and nurses in entertainment texts. On primetime sitcoms nurses are overrepresented as white women. Usually cast in secondary roles to the doctors, nurses function in TV narratives as feminine and sexualized window dressing whose primary job is to serve as sexual temptations for the doctors and surrogate mothers to the patients. Diahann Carroll's role as the mothering nurse in the title role of *Julia* and Priscilla Barnes's performance as the ditzy blond nurse Terri Alden in *Three's Company* (1977–84) are two of the most iconic performances of sitcom nurses. Prior to Reyes's Carla, the only major depiction of a Latina nurse was Ada Maris (Gina Cuevas), a stereotypically homesick Latina immigrant character on NBC's *Nurses* (1991–94). True to expected sitcom storylines about Latinas, Cuevas becomes pregnant and eventually marries the father, who is a doctor in the hospital, in the show's final season.

Challenging Whiteness

As the comedic straight character on *Scrubs*, Reyes as Carla challenged generic conventions of Latinas in TV comedies (see figure 1). Cast as a Latina character with darker skin complexion, curly hair, and an urban accent whose role centers on a career outside of the family, Reyes's Carla works against Latina typecasting and the Latin look. In the show, Reyes's character rarely engages in silly dialogue, and she rarely performs slapstick comedy. When the character is engaged in absurd behaviors, it is usually for serious effect. For instance, in the season 3 premiere "My American Girl," Carla is depicted as flaunting her sexual history with a doctor to make Turk jealous. Yet, Carla's ultimate motivation is to blackmail the recalcitrant doctor into providing a medically necessary diagnostic test for one of J.D.'s (Zach Braff) patients. Throughout the show's run Carla is represented as a vital and respected member of the medical staff. The performance of Carla's facial and body language reaffirms the character's emotionally sincere and ethically moral core. Reyes credits her realistic performance of the "no bones, no bull" attitude of Carla's character to her observation of nurses, including her twin sister (Felts 2011). Carla's character enhances the complex comedic tenor of *Scrubs*, a tenor that seamlessly moves between moments of surreal comic absurdity and emotionally deep human drama. Reyes's performance also allows the other actors the space to engage in more conventional comedic devices in a realistic hospital sitcom where life-and-death decisions are routinely made. Enhancing the show's writing with her own observational knowledge of nursing, Reyes and the writers craft a character who exploits the documented tensions between experienced nurses, newly minted medical interns, and resident doctors for

Figure 1. Judy Reyes / *Scrubs*

laughter instead of making the Latina character's ethnicity, gender, and sexuality the butt of the joke.

For example, in the pilot episode ("My First Day" 2001), audiences are introduced to Carla in the emergency room where she is wheeling in a patient and condescendingly instructing the new skittish intern J.D., whom she nicknames the feminized name "Bambi." As is typical in the first five seasons of the show, Reyes is costumed in loose-fitting medical scrubs, comfortable shoes, natural-looking makeup, and unprocessed curly hair (see figure 1). Her character's professional identity is visually emphasized instead of her gender, sexual, ethnic, and racial attributes. Reyes's performance in her first substantial scene on the show reinforces the medical competence of the character and the respect she is afforded by the most demanding doctor on the show, chief attending physician Dr. Cox (John C. McGinley). In the scene, Dr. Cox, who holds an unrequited romantic affection for Carla, flirts with her while ignoring the new intern J.D.

> *J.D. makes a move (to insert an IV), but CAN'T DO IT. Dr. Cox notices.*
> DR. COX: Time's up. Carla, would you do it for him, please? I'm also going to need an A. B. G.
> J.D.: Why are you telling her?
> DR. COX: Shut up and watch.
> CARLA: Awwww, be nice to Bambi!
> DR. COX: This Gomer has got to stop trying to die while I'm eating my lunch.
> J.D. *(under his breath)*: That's a little insensitive.
> *Dr. Cox looks up J.D.*

J.D. *(VO, thunder sounds)*: Mistake.

DR. COX: This man's 92 years old and has full dementia. He doesn't even know we're here. For Christ sake, he's inches from Carla's rack and he hasn't even flinched.

CARLA *(sincerely)*: That's so sweet.

DR. COX *(nodding)*: Yeah, it is.[6]

This scene illustrates the merging of motherly and sensuous characteristics that Lawrence envisioned for the development of Reyes's character. It sets up the character as sexy, highly skilled, and respected by the doctors and as one of the few characters not intimidated by Dr. Cox. Additionally, as envisioned by Lawrence in the pilot script, the character is depicted as holding informal and maternal authority over the new medical interns. Throughout the run of the show, the depiction of Carla shifts from authority over the interns to mentor and friend. The comedic development of Carla is never dependent on the typical Hollywood trope of the Latin female clown, nor is her black, Dominican body hypersexualized for comedic effect (Mills 2009). Instead Reyes's character occupies an unconventional space of privilege and power on the program. By casting Reyes in this role, the producers unsettle audience cognitive expectations about ethnic and minority characters, the actors who portray Latina/o characters, and the relationship between characters of color and the white leads of most TV programs.

In *Scrubs*, Braff, a white-male actor, occupies the lead role, but the acting and writing of Reyes's character produces a powerful counter-role disruptive of dominant comedic representations of race, ethnicity, class, and gender. Sitcoms traditionally depend on audiences' implicit understanding of ethnic, racial, and gender hierarchies in U.S. society, an inequality usually reproduced in the representation of relationships between the characters and reinforced through humor. Historically, the laugh track signaled to audiences the social and cultural power of the lead, typically a white man. However, as television scholar David Gillota (2013) observes, where most U.S. sitcoms "(display) the genre's uneasy relationship with race and ethnicity, *Scrubs* tackles racism, sexism and heterosexism without ignoring or comfortably resolving the conflict over the plot of one show" (120).

Reyes's character allows the writers to challenge dominant TV representations of middle-class whiteness and white heteronormative privilege in a socially conscious but not socially disruptive manner.

Together the dialogue and storylines produce a character whose immigrant working-class Afro-Latina identity breaks with normative casting practices regarding women and ethnic and racial minorities on primetime TV. As the comedic straight man, Reyes's performance provides a compelling critique of race and class privilege. Indeed, especially during the early seasons of the show, the character is usually set up in the script as a satirical check on the white and class privilege of the doctors. For example, in a first-season scene between Carla, Laverne Roberts (Aloma Wright), and J.D. ("My Best Friend's Mistake" 2001), the writing calls upon audiences' familiarity with media stereotypes of women of color to satirize them. In the scene, J.D., who is frustrated by the amount of time his best friend and roommate Turk (Donald Faison) is spending with Carla, throws nonverbal attitude, or shade, at her. Carla responds with the following:

> CARLA *(amused look)*: Bambi? Are you giving me attitude?
> *Nurse Roberts who is also behind the nurse's station walks over to stand next to Carla.*
> J.D. *(bobs his neck)*: What if I am?
> *The two nurses look at each other and laugh.*
> CARLA *(in a tone and accent reminiscent of Rosie Perez)*: Sweetie, you have to be a minority sidekick in a bad movie to pull that off.
> CARLA *(speaking to Nurse Roberts)*: You know what I'm talking about, right?
> NURSE ROBERTS: Oh, child, please!
> *The nurses exchange high fives.*
> NURSE ROBERTS: You speak the truth!
> CARLA: Explain it to this man, please.
> *Nurse Roberts wags her finger at J.D.*
> CARLA *(bobbing her head and wagging her finger)*: First, you do the head, then you do the finger, then you talk through the nose.
> *Nurse Roberts snaps her fingers.*

CARLA *(bobbing her head, hands on her waist and wagging a finger)*: And then you give a lot of attitude. That's how it works. But if you're not from here, you don't understand, so I'm not gonna even "axe" you.

J.D.: Okay, I'm gonna leave now.

CARLA *(gasping with exasperated facial expressions)*: What? Oh, no you didn't! Where you goin? Where you goin!?[7]

The humor in this scene is clever. It calls on audiences to acknowledge their own familiarity with stereotypical representations of Latinas and invites them to laugh at Reyes's parody of the dominant regime of representation for Latina and African American actors, a regime that more often than not characterizes them as uneducated, quick-tempered, working-class, and urban. Reyes's impeccably delivered tongue-in-cheek performance draws a contrast with Braff's more awkward performance of his character, thus allowing the writers and actors to comically highlight the whiteness and class privilege of the lead character.

Producing Racial Discomfort

This type of writing and character development differs from the racial and gender conventions of traditional sitcoms where characters of color in predominantly white shows usually serve as the source and target of ethnic and racial humor. Ethnic and racial minority characters rarely have the narrative opportunity to symbolically exert power against the white lead characters. Reyes as actor and Carla as character have both agency and voice to do so in *Scrubs*. For example, in the previous scene the writing and Reyes's clever performance produces a satirical undressing of a respected television archetype—the white male doctor. Carla/Reyes and Roberts/Wright's communal response, the shared response of two women and nurses of color, also creates a rare TV visual of women's interracial bonds. It is a bond rarely depicted in the narrative racial conventions of television, where minority characters are often tokens disconnected from other characters or communities of color and whose scripted lives take place in segregated and predominantly white spaces. Even the groundbreaking series *Black-ish* often reproduces this racially isolationist narrative. The writing of the characters and the performance by the actors in *Scrubs* actively ask its audience to marshal its shared collective knowledge of gender and racial TV tropes to produce the humor in Carla's disciplining of J.D.'s gender, class, and racial privilege. Carla and Roberts hold the comedic and narrative power in the scene, signaling that in *Scrubs* "the material it presents as funny and the groups or individuals it presents as laughable" will not reinforce preexisting social relationships (Mills 2009). Instead, the writers create a form of TV humor that revels in and reveals a carnivalesque reversal of ethnic, racial, and gender hierarchies where the women of color are the rational characters and the white characters are the butt of the joke.

As Gillota (2013) notes in his analysis of *Scrubs*, the writing and performance of ethnicity and race on the show is not always comfortable or open to easy narrative resolution. In a program that blends drama and comedy and where the writing actively works against established stereotypes and tropes, the production of racial, gender, and class discomfort is expected. Rather than look to the ethnic and racial minorities to deflate tensions, in *Scrubs* it is the white or male characters who provide the comic relief.

For example, the tension between the two leading female characters, Carla and medical intern Elliot (Sarah Chalke), drives the plot and character development throughout the first season of the show. Carla's character is depicted as threatened by Elliot's medical expertise, and Elliot's character is portrayed as unconscious of her racial and class privilege. The scripted and performed tension between them is both comedic and uncomfortable. In the pilot, a stressed and overworked Elliot responds to the sexist language of a patient. When Carla attempts to sympathize with her, Elliot makes the following remark:

> ELLIOT: Well you're certainly furthering the cause by wearing a thong to work and hooking up in the on-call room.
> *Excited, Mr. Burski (J.D.'s patient) WHEELS BACK INTO FRAME.*
> ELLIOT: Word gets around.

CARLA *(slow build)*: You talk like that. Do you even know my name?

Elliot stops and thinks for a moment, embarrassed that she can't meet Carla's challenge.

CARLA: I'm 34, I spend every second of my life either here or taking care of my mom. So, yeah, maybe I needed a little closeness. I'm sure you never had a quickie at the club, right? Or snuck some skinny, flat-butted college boy up to your sorority room, and you judge me? And my thong—I happen to think it makes my ass look good. And some days I need to feel good about something around here, and you judge me? Well, guess what. Word does get around, Ms. "Out For Herself," so you can dump on everyone here if you want; but you will not hurt me.

As she EXITS, hurt, they all stay frozen for a beat, then:

J.D.: Look at you *(Elliot)* making new friends.[8]

Having been called out for her racial and class privilege as well as her stereotypical assumptions about Carla as both a nurse and an Afro-Latina woman, Elliot remains standing in embarrassment at the nurse's station. J.D.'s character, who has witnessed the interaction, provides the implicit laugh track by sarcastically relieving the tension through poking fun at Elliot. His dialogue signals that Elliot should be the audience's target of laughter. J.D., who knows Carla's name, deflates the racial and class tension by calling attention to himself and creating a socially safe opportunity to snicker at his and Elliot's shared racial and class privilege.

Moments like this in the sitcom create a primetime opening for black and Latina audiences to critique the racial double standards applied to women of color in skilled professions. The writing makes explicit important character background information to help audiences understand Carla's comedic role as an antiexotic Latina straight man. True, the writers use Dr. Cox (who audiences find out briefly dated Carla) and her eventual husband Dr. Turk (Donald Faison) to make sexualized references to Carla. But the scripted interaction between Carla and the rest of the cast minimizes sexual or bodily references to the character, thus contributing to the sitcom's representation of a Latina character defined by social respectability. Even the writing around Dr. Cox, a caustic character who generally addressed the show's other characters with sarcasm and humorous contempt, reaffirms this construction of Carla. Dr. Cox never uses a pejorative nickname for Carla, rarely targets the character with verbal attacks, and always apologizes to her when he is socially inappropriate. The scripted interactions between Carla and the white characters clearly cue for the audience where and upon whom the comedy rests and who is targeted as the acceptable source of laughter, and it is rarely Reyes's performance of Carla. Reyes's character is one of the moral centers of the show.

Reimagining the Casting of Latinas

In developing Carla, the writers avoid the use of stock Latina stereotypes but remain in conversation with familiar tropes for developing stories around women and Latina characters on TV comedies, specifically the trope of motherhood. The writing and development of Reyes's character is defined through her legendary temper and untempered desire to mother the other characters and eventually become a mother herself. The maternal aspect of the character's development marks her in a particular racial and gendered way. Instead of depicting Carla through stereotypes typical of TV such as hypersexual, irrational, or emotional, she is constructed by the writers through the trope of the wise, moral, and self-sacrificing mother. Ultimately, throughout the series Reyes performs the role of the moral sage who often guides the interns, residents, and staff doctors through difficult personal and medical moments. Rather than reproduce the archetype of the Latina spitfire, *Scrubs*' writers play with the archetype of the Latina mother figure. Motherhood is, after all, a socially safe way to depict powerful women of color characters on TV comedies.

However, the writers' engagement with the motherhood trope does not reduce Carla to a stock comedic type. Depictions of Carla's maternal characteristics work in tension with the role of Carla as the antiexotic Latina, thus offering a complex and nuanced counter to the homogenized stereotyping and typecasting of Latinas on comedies.

The end result is a Latina character who remains rarely represented in the U.S. media. For example, Carla is portrayed as family oriented (a stereotypical Latina media trait), but she is rarely dressed in stereotypical colorful or tight-fitting clothing. Nor is Carla depicted as listening to stereotypical Latina/o music or eating Latina/o food. Although the writers represent Carla's brother Marco (Freddy Rodriguez) as unwilling to speak English, Carla is rarely shown speaking Spanish in the series. Finally, Reyes's outspoken character is not subservient or afraid to engage in confrontation with characters in more powerful positions than her at the hospital, but the producers never portray Carla as irrational, illogical, or hyperemotional. In these ways, Latina identity in *Scrubs* stands in stark contrast to the regime of representation of Latina women in U.S. post-racial era comedies, including that of Vergara on *Modern Family*.

Perhaps the clearest example of the producers' socially conscious TV representation of Latina/Dominican identity centers on the character's romantic relationship with Turk. Most U.S. media productions of Latina romantic relationships going back to the 1940s depict romantic attachments between "Latin" women and white-Anglo men (Lopez 2000). *Scrubs'* writers rewrite this history by emotionally and sexually pairing Carla with the main black character on the show. By narratively developing a long-term and nuanced relationship between Carla and Turk, the producers push against the racial and ethnic conventions of U.S. television and film where women of color are often depicted as desiring and privileging heteronormative whiteness. In the U.S. media, the general expectation in film and TV narratives is that women of color will be romantically paired with white men. Although there have been a few films that go against the trend (*Hitch*), *Scrubs* remains the only U.S. TV comedy to depict a romance between a Latina and black character. Reyes's performance and the writers' development of Carla's relationship with Turk reimagine the representational landscape for Latinas and Afro-Latinas on TV. In a media environment where white Latinas are privileged in casting and where fictional relationships between black and Latina/o people are rarely depicted, Reyes's Carla breaks dominant media depictions of Latinidad.

The specific ethnic and racial identity of the character as Dominican and Reyes's performance of the role provide the writers the opportunity to reverse representational expectations. That is, the writers challenge readings of Carla as essentially black or essentially Dominican by developing a character with a complex identity. Indeed, throughout the series, the writers consciously call attention to the U.S. media's pan-ethnic blurring of specific Latino differences and racial identities (Mexican, Puerto Rican, Dominican, etc.). In one of the program's most critically acclaimed episodes, "The Musical," for example, Carla and Turk, who have been arguing over her desire to return to nursing after the birth of their daughter, break into song and dance. Dancing to a tango rhythm, Carla challenges Turk's refusal to recognize her ethnic specificity:

> CARLA: I've had it up to here
> So let me make it very clear
> Because I swear I'll never clue you in again
> Every time that you profess
> I come from Puerto Rico—
> TURK: Yes?
> CARLA: For the last time, Turk, I'm Dominican!
> TURK: Don't make a big to-do
> I was simply testing you
> CARLA: Then why'd you tell J.D. our baby's Blaxican?

The writers' referencing of the term "Blaxican," a label for someone of Mexican and African American descent, illustrates a playful familiarity with the tensions over ethnic and racial labels and emerging mixed-race Latino identities. Once again, the musical lines assume a level of insider knowledge, familiarity with ethnic and racial labels, and knowledge of critiques of media representations of Latina identity as pan-ethnic and ambiguously white. The writing also smartly calls attention to the dominance of representations of Latina/os on TV as ethnically Mexican as well as the long-standing visibility of Puerto Rican actors in the U.S. media (e.g., Raul Juliá, Jennifer Lopez, Freddie Prinze, Benicio del Toro). By encouraging audiences to laugh at Turk's ignorance, Carla's frustration gives comedic voice to the blurring of ethnic differences in the media and the dominant representation of Latinos in the media as Mexican, Puerto Rican, or Cuban—but rarely or never Dominican. The writing and Reyes's performance strategically locate the character within the lived experience of U.S. Dominicans yet clearly outside of whiteness and blackness.

The casting of Reyes and her performance of Carla (a strong, independent, professional Afro-Dominican woman) calls self-reflexive attention to television's typecasting legacy, a legacy that privileges Latina/o actors and characters who are racially white or ethnically ambiguous. Through comedic performance, dialogue, narratives, and nuanced character development, the writers draw attention to the commodified flattening of Latinidad in the media. Reyes's performance insists that Carla be read with complexity and specificity as an Afro-Dominican woman.[9] This demand for repre-sentational complexity is one acknowledged and respected by the show's executive producer, Bill Lawrence: "They (nurses) are really strong, competent women. And Judy is a strong woman in real life. And one of the interesting things, when we are talking about interns, without a doubt you only need to hear Judy speak to find out that this is not a woman who is going to play a wallflower" (Paley Center 2002). *Scrubs'* production of ethnic and racial identity remains one of the most nuanced in TV and network comedies. Casting Reyes to play Carla illustrates the producers' desire to depict racial diversity and ethnic complexity in ways that speak to the lived experiences of Dominican, Spanish Caribbean, and Latino families in the United States, a diversity rarely represented in mainstream U.S. or Spanish-language popular culture.

Implications for Post-Racial-Era Comedies

That the complexity of U.S. Dominican/Latina lives could be turned into smart comedy in *Scrubs* hailed the potential for a new type of humor not dependent on the reinforcement of the status quo or on comedic stereotypes and narrative tropes often used by TV producers for comedic laughter. The lack of an explicit laugh track allowed for a more nuanced development of complex and diverse characters, nar-ratives, and humor, which together produced a more dramatic tenor for comedy, but the show ultimately failed to fully grasp audiences' post–September 11th demands for escapist fare. Despite its inability to keep up with mainstream audiences, *Scrubs'* successful formula for producing humor with a dramatic edge proved to network executives that audiences would tune in to programs with ethnically, racially, and sexually diverse casts at their core.

Scrubs' loyal but declining audience, which declined during the popular emergence of *The Office* and *Modern Family*, points to its post-racial era limitation. The decision by *Scrubs'* producers to develop stories and characters based on disruptions of TV sitcoms' conventional norms of whiteness and white privilege, even as Lawrence insisted the show was not about race, placed it at odds with the popular ascendance of colorblind ideology during the Obama era. By breaking with traditional sitcom narratives, stock characters, and ethnic and racial conventions, *Scrubs'* writers refused established representational schemas for Latina and African American TV characters. The writers' conscious decision to make the specificity of the characters' ethnic and racial identities important to the humor while not making ethnic and racial experiences central to its storylines worked against mainstream audience demands. Ultimately, the writers desire to produce humor that spoke back to whiteness and white privilege, and that was perhaps *Scrubs'* biggest limitation in this era of colorblind discourse and policies.

Although a critical favorite for her nuanced representations of nursing and Latina lives, Reyes's character is also one of the least liked by fans. On a Reddit.com community site devoted to Carla anti-fandom, the reasons for their dislike of Carla make clear the backlash toward the progressive, socially conscious writing of *Scrubs'* producers (Reddit 2015). The Reddit.com discussion characterizes Carla as judgmental, manipulative, and controlling of the male characters on the show, particularly Turk. While some audiences read the character as realistic and rational, others interpreted her maternal nature as aberrant and overly emotional. As one poster described the character, "Yeah it definitely makes her more human. Just a shitty human" (Reddit 2015). Underlying much of the discomfort for viewers who do not find Carla's character compelling are the expectations that as a Latina character she should be the source of humor, subservient to the white characters, and always sexually available to her heterosexual partner. Posters described the character as "controlling," "bossy," "judgmental," and "emotional" (Reddit 2015). If one comment represents best the gender and racial tension on the list, it is probably this one:

If I were to pick a "favorite" reason, it would have to be her concern that her daughter will not acknowledge her "latina heritage." I already didn't like carla as it was, but that just pushed me over the edge. I mean I understand being proud of your heritage, as long as it's silent pride, meaning you keep it to yourself. She took it overboard. I was and still am offended that she has the audacity to continue to live in the United States yet act like our history ain't shit compared to her being a dominican. Last time I checked, they were the ones swimming across the Rio Grande to come here, not the other way around. (Reddit 2015)

Ironically the poster conflates the character's Dominican identity with his or her reading of U.S. Mexican history. It is ironic because the writers consciously developed the ethnic specificity of Carla's character as Dominican in the series. The posting also speaks to discomfort with the scripted decision to work against the expected Latina stereotype—a more sexually available, less powerful, and less ethnically and racially marked woman. In other words, some audiences were uncomfortable with the creative decision, in the chapter's opening words, not to bring Carla down. By developing her as a socially acceptable representation of U.S. citizenship and black and Dominican womanhood, the writers fail to engage audiences' post-racial demands for racial and ethnic silence. The refusal to erase ethnicity and race is offensive to some audiences.

Carla's character is symbolic of the possibilities and limitations of a socially conscious comedy written to critically engage racism, sexism, and homophobia during a period of great economic, ethnic, and racial conflict. First, that a character of color, especially a Latina/o character, could be an integral member of an ensemble comedy becomes a key element of the formula for post-racial network comedies. Second, the audience backlash toward Reyes's performance speaks to the constraints regarding ethnicity, race, and characters of color in comedies. TV humor about race, ethnicity, and gender may be funny, but the contemporary effectiveness of the comedy depends on a colorblind performance of ethnicity, race, and Latina/o identity, a performance that does not call attention to the continuing racial and ethnic tensions. In other words, the comedy in *Scrubs* is too explicitly racial and not colorblind enough for contemporary audiences, a lesson successful post-racial era comedies have learned to avoid or cleverly negotiate.

HIPSTER RACISM COMES TO COLORBLIND TV

MICHAEL: *This is a color-free zone.*
MICHAEL TO STANLEY: *Stanley, I don't think of you as another race.*
MR. BROWN: *I'm glad you said that. We don't have to pretend that we are colorblind.*

EXCERPT FROM *THE OFFICE*'S "DIVERSITY DAY"

The humor in post-racial era comedies depends on writing that exploits audiences' commonsense acceptance of colorblind ideology even as it foregrounds the racism, sexism, and homophobia that underlies it. This chapter engages in conservative readings of the relationship between the scripting of colorblind ideology and the comedy of hipster racism on television. Chapter 3 turns to the critique of inequality potentially embedded in scripting colorblind TV content. One of the best examples of colorblind ideology at play in the writing, casting, and performance of a program in the post-racial television era is ABC's *Modern Family*. The success of *Modern Family* is indebted to the post-racial historical moment discussed in the introduction, the changing racial conventions around casting and character development outlined in chapter 1, and the ideological legacy of colorblindness in family sitcoms. From *Scrubs*, it built on the visual realism of the single-camera format, multicultural ensemble casting, and ethnic character development. From *The Office*, it borrowed the mockumentary (mock documentary) format and the use of hipster racism in comedic writing to draw in a diverse set of audiences.[1] And from the family sitcoms of earlier eras—*Leave it to Beaver* (1953–67), *I Love Lucy* (1951–57), and *Married . . . with Children* (1987–97), among others—it paid homage to the colorblind centrality of white heteronormative family life in the comedic imaginary of mainstream U.S. audiences.

But perhaps the biggest note of gratitude should be paid to the post-racial context that defined the production and reception of *Modern Family*'s comedy. In the wake of post–September 11th television's call to escapist realism and the ethnic, racial, and gender anxieties exacerbated by the global recession (2007–10), the mockumentary format in TV comedies became a popular device for delivering edgy humor to mainstream audiences. As a sitcom format popularized during the Obama era, mockumentaries also played a unique role in normalizing the comedy of hipster racism or equal-opportunity offending. Because the economic imperatives of commercially supported network television are heavily connected to advertisers' continuing demands for young, wealthy, white audiences/consumers, hipster racism in post-racial era network TV is an effective comedic tool for allowing producers to walk the fine line between maintaining majority-white audiences and attracting ethnic and racial minority viewers. To do so, post-racial era comedies like *Modern Family, Parks and Recreation,* and others engage in multicultural ensemble casting that plays with or against ethnic and racial stereotypes through comedic writing grounded in colorblindness, interpretative ambiguity, and hipster racism. In this chapter, I examine the character development and writing in *The Office* and *Modern Family,* using them as examples of colorblind ideology, interpretative ambiguity, and hipster racism in post-racial era TV comedies.

Why *Modern Family*?

Modern Family centers on the daily, interconnected lives of the extended Jay Pritchett (Ed O'Neill) family clan: Pritchett's much younger Colombian immigrant wife, Gloria (Sofía Vergara); their biological son, Joe (Pierce Wallace/Jeremy Maguire); and Gloria's son, Manny (Rico Rodriguez). The program's most traditional family features Jay's son-in-law, Phil Dunphy (Ty Burell); his daughter, Claire (Julie Bowen); and their two daughters, Haley (Sarah Hyland) and Alex (Ariel Winter), and son, Luke (Nolan Gould). The least traditional family is that of Jay's gay son, Mitchell (Jesse Tyler Ferguson); his partner, Cameron (Eric Stonestreet); and their adopted Vietnamese daughter, Lily (Aubrey Anderson-Emmons). To the showrunners these three families symbolize their take on modern family life.

Modern Family was originally titled *My American Family,* which both references and satirizes PBS's 1973 television documentary *An American Family,* a weekly broadcast focused on the Loud family. *An*

American Family is generally considered to be the first reality television program and the first television program to depict an openly gay man. Using documentary-style editing and camerawork, including the use of interviews, *Modern Family* is a comedic "real" take on white, middle-class, heteronormative family life in the twenty-first century.

According to the Nielsen ratings, *Modern Family* premiered as a top-twenty-five TV program and top three among new shows (TV by the Numbers 2010). By the end of its 2010–11 season, *Modern Family* was renewed for a third season, sold into syndication, and became the most popular situation comedy on U.S. television for that year, beating out CBS's *Two and a Half Men* (2003–15) and *Big Bang Theory* (2007–Present). In 2017 Sofía Vergara was named the world's highest-paid TV actress at $41.5 million in endorsements plus television and film income, making her the highest-paid television actress in U.S. history (Berg 2017). In its seventh season (2015–16), the show remained among the top-ten scripted television shows (Porter 2015). The success of *Modern Family* revitalized interest in the family sitcom post–September 11th, leading to the 2014 premiere of a bumper crop of ethnically and racially diverse family sitcoms, such as *Fresh Off the Boat* (2014–Present), focused on the life of a Chinese American family in 1990s Orlando; *Black-ish*, (2014–Present), which features the life of a contemporary middle-class black family in Los Angeles; and *Speechless* (2016–Present), a sitcom about a family with a special-needs teenager.

Modern Family's Nostalgic Legacy

The family sitcom is the longest-running and most conservative television genre. Beginning in the 1950s during the Golden Age of network television, family sitcoms like *The Adventures of Ozzie & Harriet* (1952–65) and *Father Knows Best* (1954–60) dominated the airwaves, defining the genre's conventions until the 1970s. Successful family sitcoms predominantly depicted the domestic lives of white, upper-middle-class, heterosexual families. The stories in these programs privileged the political status quo and the cultural and social values associated with normative heterosexual family life (Spigel and Mann 1992; Spigel and Curtin 1997). There are a few notable exceptions in the 1970s, 1980s, and 1990s such as *Good Times* (1974–79), featuring a working-class black family; *The Jeffersons* (1975–85), featuring an up-from-the-ghetto family living on New York's Upper East Side; *Roseanne* (1988–97), featuring a working-class white family; *The Cosby Show*, featuring an upper-middle-class black family; and *George Lopez*, featuring a middle-class U.S. Cuban-Mexican family.[2] Yet even sitcoms like *The Cosby Show* that did not feature a white family still maintained the genre's colorblind values and normative upper-middle-class values. Television scholar Joanne Morreale (2003) observes that *The Cosby Show* "marked a return to the 1950s model of the comfortable middle-class family, with trivial problems typically resolved at the end of the episode. The Huxtable family, with two well-educated professional parents and five well-adjusted children, happened to be black, a significant departure from the all-white families of the 1950s sitcoms, as well as from the negatively charged images of other black families seen on television" (xviii). Situating *Modern Family* within this legacy is important for understanding the show's Latina/o representations during the postracial TV era. In many ways, the narrative formula of *Modern Family* mirrors the legacy of family sitcoms in its ideological commitment to the nuclear family ideal (two working parents, one stay-at-home parent, and children).

Modern Family premiered at the height of the Great Recession (2007–10), a moment when U.S. households across the racial spectrum were facing massive unemployment, a mortgage crisis, and sharp increases in the poverty rates, particularly for African American and Latina/o families. The show's premiere in 2009 with its depiction of idealized nuclear family life provided a much-needed salve to the national and global economic wounds. *Modern Family's* extended Pritchett family live and love in an economically secure and emotionally stable white upper-middle-class environment. The plots focus on the "normal" everyday travails of modern family life (smart televisions, helicopter parents, gay children). Economic stability was presented as a cultural antidote to the financial anxieties of its audience, a comedic safe haven from the stories in the daily news. Like most U.S. family sitcoms, *Modern Family's* writers created a world without the economic or social context of life outside of the screen: a fictional world free from ethnic and racial conflict, layoffs, unemployment and stagnant wages for white men, tanking stock and housing markets, and unprecedented rates of housing foreclosures. Instead, the economic and patriarchal stability of the Pritchett family provided an escape from the chaos. In an ironic note, the Great Recession disproportionately affected California where the show takes place, but the realities of the outside world rarely appeared on the show. The economic reality of modern U.S. family life was ignored by television producers eager to return to the feel-good family comedy of a bygone TV era (Molina-Guzmán 2014).

Like traditional family sitcoms before the post-racial network era such as *Arrested Development* (2003–6) and *Malcolm in the Middle* (2000–2006), *Modern Family*'s storylines center on the domestic realm inside the family and the home rather than the public world of economics and politics. The show's claim to modernity is not a re-visioning of the contemporary family as a white, heterosexual, patriarchal institution. Instead what is modern about the show is its engagement with colorblind ethnic misunderstandings, uncomfortable negotiations with sexual difference, and the technological and moral divide between generations. For the Pritchett family, like the Huxtables, life happens in a social, political, and economic bubble where the things that truly matter are the affairs of the home and heart. Ethnic, racial, gender, and sexual differences within the family are safely contained within stories affirming the social role and cultural power of the normative family and traditional Judeo-Christian values, even though some of the families depicted in *Modern Family* are more diverse than the ones in U.S. primetime family sitcoms of the past. By using colorblind humor to elide the ethnic, racial, and sexual tensions of contemporary U.S. life, the characters and script of *Modern Family* reinforce the post-racial belief that these conflicts are irrelevant relics of a bygone era. Erasing modern conflicts from the show produces a space where targeting minorities through racially and ethnically questionable humor becomes socially acceptable.

Normalizing Hipster Racism

Modern Family's premiere months after Obama's inauguration marked the normalization of hipster racism in the post-racial TV era. As discussed in the introduction, Obama's election was used as commonsense "evidence" for long-standing claims by conservatives that the United States was finally a colorblind society that no longer required racial atonement through equity policies and civil rights laws. Obama's election resulted in political retrenchment around civil rights even as the United States witnessed the emergence of new identity-based social movements for civil rights: the Black Lives Matter movement in response to racial bias in policing and the immigration rights movement calling for the equal treatment of immigrants and migrant laborers. It was also during this time period (2001–10) that continued spikes in hate crimes against ethnic, racial, sexual, and religious minorities and immigrants were reported by the Federal Bureau of Investigation (2016).[3] News coverage of ethnic and racial conflict, especially TV news, produces an interesting visual contradiction between the evidence of ethnic and racial inequality and the colorblind ideology of scripted TV. Despite increased social and political tensions around ethnic, racial, and sexual difference in the U.S. evening news, contemporary conflicts surrounding inequality are all but invisible in primetime network programming, with the exception of more recent shows like *Black-ish*, *Brooklyn Nine-Nine*, and *The Carmichael Show* (2015–17). When ethnic and racial tensions are visible, political readings are undermined through the comedy of hipster racism. In post-racial era network comedies such as *The Office* and *Modern Family*, this hipster racism manifests itself in colorblind writing that makes all characters, regardless of identity, the targets of socially inappropriate humor.

The next section explores the role of multicultural ensemble casting and character development on the production and scripting of hipster racism. In particular, it focuses on how the writing reaffirms stereotypic discourses about racial and ethnic minorities by making Latin/a American (Latina/o and Latin American) actors and characters safe comedic targets. Whereas *Scrubs'* producers worked within a more progressive premise that was explicitly critical of racism, sexism, and homophobia, post-racial TV productions dabble in racism, sexism, and homophobia with a tongue-in-cheek approach that obfuscates their continued existence in the contemporary United States.

The Office: Making Racism Hip

To understand the success of colorblind comedy and hipster racism in *Modern Family*, it is useful to take a look at its predecessor and four-year contemporary *The Office*.[4] Television comedy is by nature economically conservative with executives copying successful genres and formulas rather than engaging in untested innovation (Gitlin 2000). At a 2010 Paley Center event, one of *Modern Family*'s executive producers, Dan O'Shannon, explained the tension: "Comedy is hard. They [executives] want to gamble their money on something that's worked before. The ones on the network side would be good in ways that you have seen before. And the ones on the writer side would be good in ways that you never imagined. It's a business and a gamble. It does old and classic things in this new and shiny way. It's unique and familiar." While providing a new representation of U.S. family life, *Modern Family* borrowed much from its successful predecessor NBC's *The Office*, as the first U.S.-produced TV comedy to effectively use a mockumentary format and colorblind humor.

A few months before the premiere of *Modern Family*, *The Office* continued its increase in the Nielsen ratings as *Scrubs* fell out of the top one hundred shows in its final 2009 season. Throughout its eight-year run, *The Office* would maintain its spot as one of NBC's most profitable and highest-rated scripted comedies. Unlike the writers of *Scrubs*, who consciously created moments of audience discomfort even as they balanced those moments with surreal comedy, *The Office*'s writing staff engaged race, ethnicity, gender, and sexuality to produce cringeworthy moments that limited potential audience and advertiser discomfort. The unwillingness of *Scrubs'* producers to simplify narratives and abandon its more progressive, socially conscious character development (elements popular with its young and highly educated niche audience) made it difficult for network executives to program the show, eventually leading to its termination.[3] Instead, the producers of *Modern Family* built on *The Office*'s formula to reimagine the family sitcom in the post-racial era of TV programming. This section examines four key elements of *The Office*'s formula: multicultural casting, absent laugh track, colorblind humor, and the writing of hipster racism.

Multicultural Casting

In the post-racial television era, television producers and network executives create the appearance of a commitment to ethnic and racial diversity through the use of multicultural ensembles and colorblind casting practices. Not surprisingly, in *The Office*, the ensemble cast consisted of gay, Latino, black, and Asian American characters. These practices allow producers the opportunity to push the boundaries of what is considered socially acceptable humor around ethnicity, race, gender, and sexuality on network television (Bonilla-Silva and Ashe 2014). Thus, the diversity and progressive casting of the show insulate the network, producers, and advertisers from accusations of racism, sexism, or homophobia. By engaging in multicultural ensemble casting, the producers create the perception of equality and inclusion in casting even though the production of the show and the overall programming of the network remains white and male.

In comparison to the exclusively white writing staffs of most TV programs, the production team of *The Office* employed the improvisational skills of the diverse actors, writers, and writing consultants. Mindy Kaling (Kelly Kapoor) received significant writing credit for a majority of the episodes, and she played an instrumental role in developing the Asian model minority type originally envisioned by the producers into a more complicated representation of Asian American identity. The producers also encouraged the actors, who were cast in part because of their improvisational skills, to shape the development of the characters and the on-screen interactions and relationships. Thus, the diversity of the writing staff and the actors' improvisational skills were an important component for producing laughter without a laugh track.

However, the diversity of *The Office*'s cast did serve as more than a multicultural marker of difference and inclusion. The diverse casting becomes central to the show's humor as it allows the writers to produce a perverse form of socially conscious comedy. Kristen Warner (2015) argues that the goal of progressive color-conscious casting is to create narratives grounded in the complexities of ethnic and racial specificities and experiences unique to the individual cast member—for example, the narratives created for Reyes on *Scrubs*. Instead, *The Office*'s writers use the ethnic and racial specificities of the characters to produce ethnic, racial, gender, and sexual humor that never calls into question white norms of civility and privilege.

The lack of canned laughter in post-racial era comedies such as *The Office* and *Modern Family* creates a "colorblind screen," enabling the comedy of hipster racism, a form of scripted humor that accommodates simultaneous and contradictory calls to racial, ethnic, gender, and sexual difference and bias (Doane 2014, 31). Not using a laugh track allowed *Scrubs* to enhance the dramatic elements of the setting alongside surreal comedic effects. Instead, *The Office*'s producers use the documentary camera and comedic timing to create a silent laugh track for the workplace comedy. Filmed without a laugh track and in an actual abandoned office building, the first season enhanced the "documentary" narrative and feel that was central to the success of its BBC predecessor. The humor becomes dependent on audiences reading or recognizing the "realness" of character types, spaces, and places that are presumably familiar to them. Ken Kwapis, a director of *The Office*, explains: "One of the things we wanted to do was give the show the sense that it was about real people in a real space. So we made the walls in such a way that they couldn't be removed. As a director or camera person, you were forced to respect the limitations of the physical space" (Burns and Schildhause 2015b). The camera work and lack of a laugh track enabled cuing the "realistic," a type of silent laugh track. The silence created the opportunity for the writers to foreground ethnic and racial difference as well as racism, sexism, and homophobia without ever decentering the white heteronormative perspective of the show.

Taking a closer look at *The Office* episode that the creators and writers credit with setting the series' comedic tone illustrates the work of the colorblind screen in creating post-racial laughter. Producer Greg Daniels identified "Diversity Day" (2005) as the adaptation's true pilot: "When I was making my first notes on adapting the show, it felt like the biggest, sweetest, low-hanging fruit for a show about a boss and a workplace in America, that had sensitivity issues, was going to be race relations. I thought that was bigger here than it was in England, because of our country's history. I was considering doing that as the pilot. I thought it would be really good" (Burns and Schildhause 2015b). In this episode, the entire office staff must undergo diversity training to legally address the racially insensitive behavior of its manager and lead character, Michael (Steve Carell). Larry Wilmore, an African American actor and writer who consulted on the episode, performed the role of the company's human resource representative, Mr. Brown.

After the training session is completed, Michael refuses to sign the company's form acknowledging his attendance. Instead he responds by creating his own diversity training program. Michael's program begins with him sharing his ethnic and racial background, expecting the others to do the same. When the staff refuses to participate, he calls on them:

> MICHAEL: Oscar, you want to go next?
> OSCAR: Both of my parents were born in Mexico.
> MICHAEL: What part?
> OSCAR: Mexico City. They moved to the United States the year before I was born.
> MICHAEL: Great story. American dream. Now, is there another term you like to use, besides "Mexican?" Something less offensive.
> OSCAR: Mexican isn't offensive.
> MICHAEL: It has certain . . . connotations.
> OSCAR: Like what?
> MICHAEL *(trapped)*: Like . . . I don't know.
> OSCAR *(getting a little heated)*: What are the "connotations," Michael.
> MICHAEL: Okay, remember. Honesty, Empathy, Respect . . .[6]

Carell's facial expressions and deadpan delivery as well as the absence of a laugh track is key to the humor as both reinforce the depiction of Michael's "innocent" lack of racial awareness, an implicit and sometimes explicit form of prejudice that only this character exhibits in the series.

Without the laugh track, the actors' visual performances of social discomfort in response to the prejudicial statements of the white lead character enhance the comedic impact of the dialogue. Reflecting on the racial content of the episode, actor Brian Baumgartner (Kevin Malone) explains:

It was certainly an inappropriate thing for someone to do in the workplace, but the message behind that was the same message that was behind a lot of the episode. His naiveté got him in trouble, but part of what he was doing, in an age where you were so overloaded on the PC side, and nobody was able to say anything, was forcing people to examine from a naive perspective, why isn't this something we can talk about? Obviously, a work place setting is what makes everyone uncomfortable, but I think just bringing up the issue of race and not hiding is why I'm proud of it. (Burns and Schildhause 2015b)

Without the laugh track, the production of cringe comedy (comedy that makes audiences cringe with discomfort) introduces an effective level of comedic ambiguity. Audiences have to actively work to think through the delivery of the lines, physical expressions of the actors/characters, and preexisting relationships between the characters for cues on what and whom it is socially acceptable for them to laugh at. The butt of the joke is not easily marked or determined, and that ambiguity affords audiences the opportunity to laugh at Michael for his prejudiced assumptions. And it also provides audiences who might relate to and share Michael's experiences and assumptions a socially safe opportunity to laugh with him and at Oscar's discomfort. For the comedy of hipster racism in *The Office* to do the desired progressive work discussed by the writers and actors, it is dependent on the exclusive interpretation of Michael's character and actions as socially inappropriate. But the lack of a laugh track precludes this singular reading; in fact, it does the opposite and produces an open interpretation rather than a closed one.

Colorblind Humor

Given the imperative to avoid controversy and broadcast programming able to attract the largest audience possible, the social and political context in which post-racial era comedy airs is central to understanding the role of colorblind ideology. For example, the first season of *The Office* was created, produced, and broadcasted at the peak of post–September 11th ethnic and racial tensions toward immigrants. Indeed, two months after "Diversity Day" aired, the U.S. House of Representatives passed the "Sensenbrenner Bill," H. R. 4437, a bill targeting the U.S.–Mexico border and Mexican immigration as potential sites of terror. In this context, Carell's deadpan delivery and Oscar's angry but muted response potentially reinforce the show's colorblind humor, a type of comedy that depends on audiences' agreement, or at least familiarity, with the national anti-immigrant discourse and the white heteronormative values of the show. The network's censorship decisions in this episode further illustrate the social boundaries of racial humor. Greg Daniels discusses that point:

> And Michael goes on this long-run trying to say, "Well, INCEST is a good device because . . ." and Mr. Brown says, "We can't use it, it's too inappropriate." Michael says, "Well, I'll give you the reasons it's very helpful. Incest is bad. Racism is bad. Incest, we're all related, we're all brothers and sisters so racial methods, and this is a fact the states where there's a lot of racism are the states that have a lot of incest." And he goes on trying to salvage his whole idea. That didn't make it in. [laughs] Possibly for good reason. (Burns and Schildhause 2015b)

By the logic of the network's censors, it is permissible to air comedy grounded in racist views about Mexicans, but it is not acceptable to equate racism with sexual aberrance and class on the air. Within the story arc of the series, Carell's character is never demoted and rarely disciplined for his socially inappropriate and legally questionable actions.

The episode illustrates Doane's (2014) observation that colorblind ideology in U.S. popular culture depends on the ability to see skin color and understand socially appropriate behavior even as audiences ignore the significance of color, race, or ethnicity to U.S. political and cultural life. As "Diversity Day" illustrates, the joke depends on Oscar's ethnic identity as a Mexican American. The only two supporting characters originally written into the pilot were Kevin and African American office mate Stanley Hudson (Leslie David Baker). Although Nuñez is Afro-Cuban, the writers specifically developed his character as Mexican American. It may be reasonably concluded that the writers saw the actor's and character's ethnic identity as central to the production of the show. In another episode considered central to the development and success of the series, the character of Oscar, whom the writers decided to depict as a gay man after season 1, is accidentally outed by Michael ("The Gay Witch Hunt" 2006).

Colorblind humor is particularly effective for network television because it shifts social responsibility from the text and its production to the audience and its reception of the text. It is not the executives' or producers' problem, after all, if the biases of mainstream white audiences shape how they read the text. Yet, as Kristen Warner (2015) notes, colorblind ideology in U.S. popular culture depends on the everyday invisibility of white privilege, even as ethnic and racial inequalities persist. Changes in the writing of Michael's character from the first season to the third further contribute to the erasure of whiteness and white male privilege. Throughout the first three seasons, the rudeness and more explicitly racial and ethnic prejudices of Michael's character made him more culpable and less likeable to audiences. As the series progressed, Carell's depiction of Michael softened, eventually giving way to a more sympathetic, well-meaning character who through no fault of his own is an ingénue when it comes to ethnic, racial, gender, and sexual difference. Michael's character is, as Warner describes, the result of white prejudice as "rare and aberrational rather than systemic and ingrained" (8). Michael's character becomes the symbol of implicit individual bias rather than the racist production of white privilege. By the end of the series, it is the character's ridiculous behavior (and not his status as a white heterosexual man) that is the primary source of laughter. The success of The Office's comedy depends on the mainstreaming of colorblind ideology on entertainment TV.

Hipster Racism

Post-racial-era TV comedy is characterized by the absence of the laugh track and the colorblind approach to ethnic and racial difference that provide the setup for the comedy of hipster racism, a colorblind form of comedy that depends on racial, ethnic, gender, and sexual differences. Hipster racism reinforces the colorblind values even as the characters' differences are increasingly central to the production of laughter. The colorblind values of contemporary comedies together with the use of hipster racism make it possible for audiences to hold contradictory readings of television scripts, interpretations that release audiences of white guilt or social discomfort yet create a contested space of visibility and subversive pleasure for audiences of color (Doane 2014).

Returning to "Diversity Day" as an example, the ethnic, racial, gender, and sexual humor in *The Office* almost exclusively revolves around Michael's socially inappropriate behavior and beliefs and the ensemble's improvised responses or lack of responses to Michael's prejudicial assumptions about race, gender, and sexuality. The focus on Michael's individual ethnic, racial, and sexual transgressions is one of the main adaptations the U.S. writers of *The Office* made to the original British comedy. Throughout the series, the writers position Carell's character in opposition to his unwilling antagonist, the socially conscious human resource officer Toby Flenderson (Paul Lieberstein, a writer on the show). In the series, Lieberstein's subdued and apathetic Toby is routinely called in to legally intercede with regard to the racist, sexist, and/or homophobic behavior of Carell's emotionally exaggerated Michael. In the series narrative, the hostile work climate created by Carell's character is never depicted as the institutional result of white patriarchal culture and heteronormative privilege, but rather as another joke to illustrate the individual flaws of Michael Scott, the self-centered boss.

The comedic writing that surrounded Carell's character points to a key characteristic of the post-racial TV era: the normalizing of hipster racism. A central component of the normalization of hipster racism is the development of sympathetic yet socially flawed white lead characters. Using racism as a form of comedy is not a new convention. As Angela Kinsey, who played Angela on the show, recognized of "Diversity Day": "Whenever I read our scripts, there were so many that we did that were part of the cringe humor. I think Archie Bunker did that on *All in the Family*, which is a super old call-back because I'm an old lady [laughs]. But one of your lead characters is inappropriate, you get to call them out on their crap. Say, 'No, that's wrong, dude!'" (Burns and Schildhause 2015b). Evoking *All in the Family* as a referent is interesting because communication research on the program documented the way audiences read the show as both a critique of racism and as an affirmation of racist views (Wilson, Gutiérrez, and Chao 2013). The primary difference is that while the laugh track on *All in the Family* (1971–79) directly cued audiences to when it was socially acceptable to laugh, post-racial era comedies do not provide any explicit cues. In *The Office* there are no such explicit cues, and Michael's character is rarely explicitly called out for his assumptions. Indeed, most of the time his transgressions are met with silence and stares of disbelief by the characters.

Instead, the use of racism, sexism, and homophobia as humor in post-racial era comedies depends on a more ambiguous set of codes to signal socially appropriate laughter. For example, the humor around the famously improvised kiss between Carell and Nuñez is dependent on the actors' physical performance, audiences' familiarity with the narrative and character history of the show, prior knowledge of the relationship between the characters, and their own experiences and ability to relate to the characters in the scene (see figure 2). In the season 3 episode "Gay Witch Hunt," Michael is unaware of Oscar's sexual identity until Toby disciplines him for using the word "faggy." The next scene cuts to Michael's confessional interview: "I would have never called him that if I knew. You know. You don't call retarded people retards. It's bad taste. You call your friends retards when they are acting retarded. And I consider Oscar a friend." The creative decision to depict the show's lead character as equating gay people to people who are developmentally delayed is an example of the normalization of hipster racism.

Carell's emotionally sincere delivery of the potentially offensive monologue effectively produces sympathy for Michael. Where some audience members might cringe at the comedic use of the socially charged term "faggy," others might welcome the term as a critique

Figure 2. Steve Carell and Oscar Nuñez / *The Office*

of progressive demands for "political correctness." Published interviews with the show's creators, writers, and actors make clear their awareness of the social boundaries around diversity and inclusion. For audiences familiar with gray- and white-collar workplace policies regarding sexual harassment and discrimination, Carell's performance pokes satiric fun of the institutional privileging of multiculturalism. At the same time, the effectiveness of hipster racism depends on a shared agreement that the white lead character's flaws are socially innocent and not institutionally and intentionally systemic. Doing so reaffirms television comedy's commonsense logic of colorblindness as it reduces racism, sexism, and homophobia to individual pathology rather than the effect of systemic and structural inequalities.

Hipster racism in a workplace comedy provides the producers increased agency to portray socially unacceptable and legally actionable behaviors and language, and it is that cultural transgression that produces the humor. The production of hipster racism depends on scripting potentially controversial or politically risky moments of humor, such as having Michael apologize to Oscar for calling him "faggy" in front of his fellow office workers, thereby outing the socially conservative Oscar. The editing and nonverbal performances of the ensemble cast reinforce the transgressions. First, the camera cuts from Carell to observe the religious and socially conservative Angela sanitizing her hands as she glares at Oscar. Then the camera pans to Oscar's silent response of disgust and disbelief. In published interviews on the improvisational nature of *The Office*, Nuñez points to the above scene as an effective example of the ensemble's collaborations around socially inappropriate comedy. For the socially conscious humor embedded in the nonverbal interactions between the actors in this scene to work, it depends on some audiences' familiarity with homophobic stereotypes of gay men as diseased and homosexuality as physically infectious. In this reception context, Angela's display of prejudiced ignorance is the butt of the joke. But it is the silence that also produces hipster racism, or in this instance hipster homophobia. The writers' decision to make the interaction nonverbal enhances the comic ambiguity necessary to produce hipster racism or in this case hipster homophobia. In the episode's concluding interview, Oscar reveals that he was more amused than offended by Michael's public apology and that he filed a grievance against Michael for which he was compensated with paid leave. The scripting of the episode and the way that Nuñez's character ultimately benefits from being the target of homophobia further justifies post-racial values by shifting the social burden of prejudice and discrimination to the individual and highlighting the ways the system benefits and protects minorities.

Colorblind comedy produces a marketable interpretative ambiguity through contradictions in the show's writing and character development. Indeed, part of NBC's investment in *The Office* was the program's ability to bring in a young, highly educated audience, similar in profile to the *Scrubs* audience but consistently larger. Such an audience might not care about or be concerned with contemporary social norms and mores, but these audiences are at least aware of socially appropriate behavior and contemporary identity politics. It must also be recognized that audiences of post-racial era comedies are not likely to identify as white supremacists, because white supremacist audiences do not generally watch mainstream television programming (King 2014). Rather, audiences of post-racial era comedies are the type that understand hipster humor is socially inappropriate and see themselves as socially conscious, even though they may also be equally uncomfortable with changes in sexual culture, ethnic and racial demographics, and the ever-shifting terrain of identity politics in the United States. Much the way *All in the Family* did for its audience, post-racial era comedies allow white audiences to laugh at or even sympathize with racist, sexist, or homophobic language and behavior as these are normalized as the result of individuals' inability to adjust to the "new" mores of a more socially conscious culture.

Hipster Racism and Latinas

The Office's successful blend of multicultural ensemble casting, silent laugh track, colorblind humor, and hipster racism holds a lasting influence on post-racial era comedy aired after 2009. Greg Daniels, the producer of *The Office*, created NBC's *Parks and Recreation*. Dan Harmon tweaked the formula for NBC's *Community* (2009–15), and Steven Levitan and Christopher Lloyd extended it to family sitcoms in *Modern Family*. All of the shows except for *Modern Family* starred white lead actors. *Modern Family* pushed the envelope by costarring Sofía Vergara, a Latin/a American actor of Colombian heritage. The casting of Vergara pushed colorblind humor and the production of hipster racism in interesting ways.

A New Twist on the Latin Clown

During World War II the Hollywood film industry played an active role in soothing cultural and economic relations between the United States and Latin America through the production of "Goodwill Cinema" (López 1991). The movies, which ranged from comedies to dramas, predominantly featured Latin American women in romantic relationships with white-Anglo men. These movies gave rise to and introduced U.S. audiences to Latin American superstars such as Carmen Miranda and Dolores del Rio, and they also helped establish the Hollywood norms of typecasting Latina actors and stereotyping the characters they would perform—the sexy spitfire, treacherous dark lady, and virginal señorita (Béltran 2010; Fregoso 2003; López 1991; Mendible 2007). These cinematic performances featuring Latin/a American spitfire, or female clown, characters focused on an intercultural comedy of errors and the tensions embedded in interracial romantic relationships.[7] Over time the spitfire became a staple Hollywood Latina stereotype. A role originally created in the 1940s to make Latin/a America foreignness less threatening and more desirable for economic, cultural, and political cross-pollination continues to inform the representational legacy of post-racial era family sitcoms and Latina representations on U.S. television.

However, the post-racial era version of the modern Latin female clown is more than a one-dimensional stereotype. The Latin spitfire as depicted by Vergara has made the archetype culturally safe and familiar, and racially different and foreign. In *Modern Family*, Vergara's character is depicted as ethnic clown and idealized Latina mother. She embodies the comedic straight man of Desi Arnaz and the gendered comedic clown role of Lucille Ball. The ethnic straight man is a sitcom role dating back to Desi Arnaz in *I Love Lucy* (1951–57) and Freddie Prinze in *Chico and the Man* (1974–78) (Béltran 2010; Carini 2003). Indeed, Lucille Ball, who canonized the role of the female clown in U.S. sitcoms, is one of Vergara's icons:

I only wish to be a little bit, or anything, that people think I could be a little of bit of her (Lucille Ball). She has always been for me an icon and I used to watch her show in Colombia. In Colombia, I grew up watching her. And it's one of the things I remember, having fun watching television, is that couple. Um . . . I mean it's incredible for me to have a job like *Modern Family* that lets me be a character that is so you know so Latin, so comfortable. I think it's amazing that the creators of the show, the writers, the network had the balls to (laughter) so that they had the balls to put someone like me on television (Paley Center 2015).

Given that the spitfire role is one Latinas are asked to reprise, especially during highly contentious and socially anxious periods in U.S. history, it is not surprising that a Latina would be cast in that role during the Great Recession (Molina-Guzmán 2014).

Latina Clowns in the Age of Trump

Post–September 11th Latina visibility in television, the movies, and elsewhere has occurred in the context of political hostility toward U.S. Latina/os and Latin American and Muslim immigrants. The context of that visibility points to the cultural dangers bound in the colorblind multiculturalism of the post-racial TV era. The four years leading up to *Modern Family*'s premiere, for instance, were defined by intense conflicts over immigration in the United States. A month after Obama's 2004 election to the U.S. Senate, the U.S. House of Representatives approved H. R. 4437. Known as the "Sensenbrenner Bill," H. R. 4437 was the most restrictive immigration bill ever passed by the House. The bill, which failed in the Senate, required increased fencing along the U.S.–Mexico border, mandated federal custody for undocumented immigrants with ten-year minimum sentencing for falsified immigration documentation, and established felony charges for any U.S. citizen housing or transporting undocumented citizens. House approval of the bill led to the largest immigration rights mobilization in U.S. history informally called the "Day Without an Immigrant" marches on May 1, 2006. More than a million immigration rights protestors joined marches across the country. After Obama's first presidential election, the failed Sensenbrenner Bill inspired successful state-level anti-immigration legislation (Arizona [2010], Alabama [2011], Georgia [2011], Indiana [2011], South Carolina [2011], Utah [2011]). Donald Trump's 2015–16 campaign and presidency made building a wall along the Mexican border, renegotiating trade agreements with Mexico, and aggressively deporting undocumented immigrants centerpieces of his agenda. Although the language of these laws did not specifically target Mexican and Latin American immigrants, the racialized political intent of the legislation is clear—the dehumanization of Mexicans as symbolic stand-ins for U.S. Latina/os. Post-racial-era TV representations of Latinas and hipster racism must be read against these cultural, social, and political anxieties surrounding Latin American immigration and U.S. Latina/o populations.

The rest of this chapter examines Vergara's performance of Gloria to explore the cultural conditions that allow a Latin/a American character on network TV to become popular and a Colombian actor so marketable, especially in the anti-Latina/o context described above. In *Modern Family*, the producers made Vergara's depiction of Gloria palatable for mainstream audiences by emphasizing the visual and audible forever-foreign difference through hipster racism. Gloria was mediated in the script as a safe and modern intercultural bridge and nostalgic rerun of feel-good comedies. Vergara as Gloria is U.S. TV's modern Latin/a American goodwill ambassador, thus illustrating the effective role of colorblind humor and hipster racism.

Gendering a U.S. Colombian Spitfire

Television scholar Jason Mittell (2015) notes that actors play an integral part in the character development of TV comedies: "Television characters derive from collaboration between the actors who portray them and the writers and producers who devise their actions and dialogue. Performance is always a collaborative creative act, as actors embody the roles sketched out on the page" (119). Speaking about her role at a Los Angeles Paley Center event, Vergara (Paley Center 2010) acknowledged the centrality of her own Colombian identity and body as key elements of her exaggerated performance of ethnicity and gender: "Well it's amazing for me because I never thought I was going to find a role that is so perfect for me. To be able to be Colombian and I don't have to worry about the accent. It's fantastic." By locating the character as a Colombian woman portrayed by a Colombian woman, Vergara and the writers carefully navigate the Latina/o threat discourse prevalent in U.S. news that constructs U.S. Mexicans, and by implication U.S. Latina/os, in socially devalued ways (Chavez 2013; Santa Ana 2012).

The repeated association between the actor's and character's Colombian ethnic identity is readily reinforced by Vergara in media interviews on the scripting of her character. In an interview with *Redbook*, Vergara reflected on the influence her ethnic background had on the character: "A lot. Every time I get a script, I think, how would my mother or my aunt do it? And that's Gloria" (Dunn 2011). The slippage between the character and actress, the fictional and the real, is integral to Vergara's role and audiences' reading of Gloria. As Dustin Rowles (2014) notes of the show's success, "*Modern Family* was an instant hit, thanks in some part to the smart sensibilities of the show, and in some part to the diverse cast, which attracted an audience from a wide array of demographics." Similar to the way multicultural casting and the role of Reyes's functioned in *Scrubs*, the producers of *Modern Family* explicitly sought a Latina, like Vergara, to cast in the role Gloria. The difference is that the color-conscious comedy of *Scrubs* is replaced by the less progressive comedy of hipster racism.

The accent and the hypersexualized gendering of Vergara's Latin/a American body are the core elements in her gendered performance of Latinidad as the Colombian American spitfire. Lucila Vargas (2000) first coined the concept "gendering of Latinidad" to document the practices and technologies used in news production, practices that contribute to the feminization of the Latina/o community as a collective. Vargas concludes that the journalistic focus on personal stories about extraordinary Latina/o individuals as well as the highlighting of domestic issues related to Latina/o families genders Latina/os in ways that shape public perceptions of the community's agency and power. Because the majority of news stories about Latina/os are limited to coverage of exceptional individuals, domestic life, and heteronormative traditional family values, Latina/os are associated with archetypical feminine characteristics such as sexual fertility, domesticity, and powerlessness. Thus, Latinidad is a socially constructed category of identity explicitly connected to race and ethnicity and feminized through social and cultural institutions, such as the family and the media (Molina-Guzmán 2010; Vargas 2000). Media discourses of gender are informed by the interaction of femininity and masculinity with class, race, and ethnicity.

The Latina Body

The narrative and visual focus on the display of Gloria's body, sexuality, and domesticity recirculated already-familiar journalistic narratives. It also reaffirmed the gendered aspects of Latina typecasting and ethnic stereotyping: hot tempered, hypersexual, curvaceous, dark haired, and dark eyed. In a Tumblr post by TV writer Steven Falk, he revealed the initial casting breakdown from the *Modern Family* pilot (see figure 3). In the breakdown provided to the casting directors by the producers, the photographic image for Gloria's character depicts an actor with long dark hair in a tight-fitting red dress revealing her cleavage. The casting breakdown reads, "30s, Hispanic, beautiful, strong, quick-tempered. Protective mother. Divorced six years ago." The producers were not particularly interested in casting an actor of a specific Latina ethnicity as much as casting an actor who could physically embody their vision of the Latina type. Interestingly, the casting photo for Gloria's character in the breakdown is a whole-body shot rather than the typical head shot used by casting directors. Interestingly, Vergara has always been consciously aware of the physical expectations surrounding her body for the U.S. casting of Latina roles: "But when I started acting, I would go to auditions and they didn't know where to put me because I was voluptuous and had the accent—but I had blonde (hair)" (Mateo 2010). Vergara dyed her hair for English-language auditions and spoke often of her decision to change her hair color as central to her success in Hollywood. Gloria's physical appearance and the strategic use of her body for comedic effect produce a culturally safe articulation of Latin/a American identity on TV.

Throughout the series, the visual framing of Vergara's body by the camera, the strategic use of costuming, and the sexual associations produced by both the camera work and the costuming inform the production of comedy. Costuming is a significant production

The Pritchett - Delgado Family

Jay
60s, successful businessman, divorced. Recently married Gloria, struggles to stay "young" for her.

Gloria
30s, hispanic, beautiful, strong, quick-tempered. Protective mother. Divorced six years ago.

Manny
12ish, Gloria's son - Jay's stepson. Old soul, sensitive, passionate, a young romantic.

Figure 3. *Modern Family* original casting character breakdown

convention for communicating quick information to audiences about a character's gender, race, and ethnicity. From the pilot episode of *Modern Family* Gloria's costuming has played a central role in the comedy surrounding Vergara's character. Gloria/Vergara's body, specifically her breasts and hourglass figure, are a regular part of the comedic setups. Indeed Vergara's wardrobe on the show (and cinematic roles) is characterized by the use of bright colors, animal prints, low-cleavage dresses, tight-fitting pants, and body-fitting dresses. In a first season episode, for example, the camera cuts away to Jay, who joins a group of male guests intently staring into a bounce house ("Fizbo" 2009). The camera also takes on the role of voyeur as it films the scene through a bounce-house screen window. Gloria's body, which is clad in a black tank top, skinny jeans, and large gold hoop earrings, but not her face, bounces in and out of the camera frame. Vergara/Gloria's body becomes the visual focus of the camera's gaze. Similarly, during the first half of season four, Gloria's pregnancy clothing and her refusal to wear socially acceptable maternity clothing becomes a recurring joke (see figures 4 and 5). In one of the season's most humorous scenes, Vergara physically rips out of her colorful tight-fitting maternity clothes ("Snip" 2012). Thus, stereotypic dress is reinforced as a core element of the visual performance of Latina femininity as heterosexual, desirable, and hypersexualized.

The Spitfire Voice. Equally as important as the physical typecasting and costuming of the spitfire in television comedy is language and accent. As illustrated in *Modern Family's* casting breakdown (see figure 3), Gloria's ethnic identity, undocumented status, and accent are not listed as preferences for the role. Yet, the pilot script circulated with the casting breakdown did indicate the linguistic expectation of

Hipster Racism Comes to Colorblind TV

69

an accent. For example, the script called for Vergara to pronounce Jay's name "Yay," and in a later scene the character mixes up the order of words.

Figure 5. Sofía Vergara in green costume / *Modern Family*

Figure 4. Sofía Vergara / *Modern Family*

> JAY: I'll give him *(Manny)* one thing, he's got some cahoneys.
>
> GLORIA: Please, do not do a torture on my language.

From the show's first episode, Vergara's performance of language racializes and ethnically defines the character:

> GLORIA: We're very different. Jay's from the city, he has big business. I come from a small village, very poor, but very, very beautiful. It is the number one village in all Colombia for the . . . what's the word?
>
> JAY: Murders.
>
> GLORIA: Yes, the murders. *(Although not noted in the script, Vergara delivers the "Yes" as "Jess" with a very pronounced Spanish accent.)*

By using a familiar, racialized, ethnic accent, Vergara taps into television's representational legacies about Latinas.

Responding to questions about the stereotyping surrounding her role, Vergara has remarked in media interviews, "At the beginning, I was worried. I thought, she's a sexy woman, divorced with a kid, marrying the older guy, and she's a gold digger. How are people going to like this character? But the writers have done such a brilliant job. There hasn't been one person who's said, 'We don't believe this relationship.' Also, they've allowed me to be really Latin—you know, screaming in Spanish. And I make my accent worse" (Dunn 2011). A part of being "really Latin" for Vergara is the exaggerated accent. Vergara discussed the importance of exaggerating the use of language and accent for the role in her 2011 appearance on *Inside the Actors Studio*. The accent in combination with the scripting of grammatical errors, mistakes in vocabulary, and linguistic misunderstandings highlight her foreignness and difference from the whiteness of the other characters. Vergara's stereotyped and racialized voice becomes the comedy to be laughed at by audiences. The role of language, like the racialized sexualization of Gloria/Vergara's body, creates an exotic character, forever an outsider to the rest of the family and to the predominantly white audiences who tune in to the program. Both of these stereotypical and archetypical characteristics—physicality and language—contribute to the post-racial production of colorblind humor and hipster racism on the show.

Colorblind Comedy and Hipster Racism in *Modern Family*

Vergara's body and the actor's use of language produces a complicated type of visibility that enables the production of colorblind humor and hipster racism. The popularity of the actor and the character raises an interesting set of questions about the progressive possibilities for Latina visibility, at least on network sitcoms, during the contemporary era. For instance, the setup in the episode "Open House of Horrors" (2012) illustrates the double-edged scripting of hipster racism and the explicit evocation of Vergara's ethnicity:

WHITE MALE PARTY ATTENDEE (*The attendee is wearing a baby carrier with a sack of sugar in it.*): I love when people put some thought into their outfit. Illegal alien, sugar daddy.

GLORIA *(Dressed in a shiny, green latex body suit with antennas. Replies angrily)*: Why do you say "illegal"?

PARTY GUEST: Because antennas are alien, and you're . . .

VERGARA INTERUPTS: What? Illegal? Because of the color of my skin? Why don't I dump your baby in your gas tank?

JAY: Gloria!

JAY *(speaking to the guest)*: Uh, no hard feelings, please. Just enjoy the party, okay?

JAY *(speaking to Gloria)*: First of all, relax. We're at a party. Secondly, you've been deported twice. You are not allowed to be that defensive.

The scene illustrates the typical gendered and racialized characteristics used by the writers to portray Gloria—sexualized clothing, linguistic misunderstanding, quick temper, loud, and emotional. It also demonstrates the complicated role of hipster racism on a show celebrated for its diversity. In the scene, *Modern Family*'s writers consciously use the socially loaded term "illegal alien" much in the same way *The Office* writers played with the word "faggy." Because the hypervisibility of Vergara's character is already written in the script through a recurring set of gendered stereotypes, the dialogue and storylines about pregnant Gloria's increasingly irrational behavior further racialize the character. In particular, the script's foregrounding of Gloria's undocumented past through the use of what is considered by many U.S. Latina/os to be a pejorative term ("illegal alien") demonstrates the producer's keen understanding of hipster racism or the implicit use of racism and xenophobia to create laughter.

The guest is presumed to be socially "colorblind" to Gloria's ethnic difference. Thus, his response and Jay's subsequent disciplining of Gloria work against the character's claims of discrimination. In the scene, Jay's character, as he so often does, embodies the normative voice of white civility, reason, and rationality. Colorblind humor in post-racial era TV depends on these narratives of white civility to discipline disorderly interruptions by brown bodies and voices. By making the brown people a source of acceptable laughter, hipster racism normalizes socially inappropriate, racist, and sexist interpersonal interactions.

Another example of the writers' use of language to produce hipster racism is a recurring joke in the second season regarding Gloria's anger at the family for making fun of her spoken English ("Halloween" 2010). The writers' decision (and Vergara's ability) to draw attention to the actor's ability to speak fluent unaccented English draws focus to the racialized role of language in the comedy:

> GLORIA (*speaking in exaggerated standard English to Cameron while Claire stands by*): Claire just doesn't understand, Cam. Maybe she's never been picked on for being different.
> CLAIRE: When, Gloria? When have you ever been picked on for "being different"?

Claire's exasperated reaction and dialogue undercut Gloria's attempt to garner sympathy for her experiences of discrimination and desire for intercultural acceptance. The dialogue, lack of a laugh track, and implicit scripted references to Gloria's identity produce hipster racism by disrupting the social cues for audiences regarding who and what it is okay to laugh at in this scene.

Other times, however, racism and xenophobia are more explicit in the writing of the post-racial era comedy of *Modern Family*. For instance, in "The Incident" (2009) Claire and Mitchell recount their mother's (Dede) behavior at Jay and Gloria's wedding. Jay's ex-wife, Dede (Shelley Long), makes a toast referring to Gloria as Charo, the iconic Latina spitfire icon of the 1970s. In the toast, Dede drunkenly states, "To the bride and the groom, my ex, thirty-five years we were together. Seriously, I knew they were perfect for each other when I saw his wallet and her boobs." The scripted comedy in this scene plays to and against stereotypic assumptions that an older, wealthy, and white man could ever authentically love an ethnic woman or that a young, sexually attractive ethnic woman could ever really love an older white man. Long's dialogue and performance of white feminine victimhood reinforce the producers' construction of Gloria as perpetually outside of white normativity and the socially acceptable standards of upper-middle-class femininity.

Similar to Latin/a American spitfires of Hollywood's past, Vergara's racially white appearance and slapstick acting, along with the cringe-worthy writing of hipster racism in *Modern Family*, produce a character who is ideologically safe for audiences to consume, particularly during a moment of heightened racial and ethnic anxiety in the United States. The producers are conscious of the sexual and racial borders that limit the representation of diversity on the show. Discussing the role of Gloria at a 2010 Paley Center event, *Modern Family* writer and producer Dan O'Shannon reflected on the constraints surrounding the character's development: "And it also helps that we have never showed Jay and Gloria kiss because America is not ready for that." By O'Shannon's logic, U.S. audiences are okay with a modern rendition of the Latin spitfire, but audiences, advertisers, and network censors are not ready for a visual depiction of intercultural and intergenerational Latina love and sexuality on primetime TV. Pointing to the limits of representations of intergenerational and intercultural relationships, the writers in the sixth season of *Modern Family* legally marry Cameron and Mitchell. It is presumably less controversial to depict a gay wedding than to let Gloria and Jay kiss on network TV. The cultural constraints under which the writers portray the Gloria–Jay relationship are also interesting. Gloria remains the only parent to be financially dependent on her spouse. In doing so, Gloria remains subservient to her second, much-older and wealthier husband, consequently reinforcing the heteronormative patriarchal whiteness at the ideological center of post-racial era comedies like *Modern Family*. Because the ethnic character marries into, rather than earns, her economic access to the American Dream, Gloria's social status within the family is tenuous and the perpetual source of family tension and conflicts. *Modern Family*'s comedy throws back to a nostalgic and conservative take on white heteronormative family life and values.

The production of colorblind comedy and hipster racism taps into broader U.S. discourses about what it means to be a socially acceptable "model minority." Thus, the producers of post-racial era comedies develop characters rarely seen on television, but only as those characters' happiness reinforces the norms and values of white heterosexual familial domesticity.

The Nuances of Hipster Racism

In post-racial era comedy, the burden of arbitrating racism, sexism, and homophobia on TV is placed on the subjectivities of the audience rather than the intent of the producers. Without the laugh track providing audible cues to the joke, audiences laugh sympathetically with the racist experiences of ethnic and racial minority characters or sympathetically with the white characters' continual need for intercultural translation to understand the differences that have entered their white upper-middle-class lives. Hipster racism in post-racial era comedy blurs the lines of socially appropriate behavior without calling into question white privilege. It is worth requoting TV scholar Brett Mills here: "[Y]ou can only be offended by a joke if you perceive it to be a joke, albeit one that you don't find funny. [. . .] This means you need to understand the cues which signal the text's comic intention while simultaneously finding such humour inappropriate; to not accept the cue is to render the moment serious, or worse, incomprehensible" (2009, 94–95). Post-racial comedies depend on the ambiguity surrounding the joke. In the absence of traditional sitcom conventions such as the laugh track that cue the joke and affirm for audiences the social consensus around U.S. norms, beliefs, and values regarding ethnic and racial difference, racism, sexism, and homophobia become subject to interpretation. The responsibility for producing nonoffensive content shifts away from the writer and makes audiences the social, ethical, and moral arbiters of socially acceptable humor.

There is a subtle complexity in TV's production of hipster racism. In *The Office*, for example, Oscar always performed the role of the comedic straight man by drawing attention to the absurdity of the actions and dialogue of the white characters around him. Oscar's character, an Afro-Mexican gay male accountant, could have been the biggest stereotypic clown on the show (i.e., Sean Hayes in the role of Jack on *Will & Grace* [1998–2005, 2017–Present]). Instead, he actually became the antiexotic Latino or as one blogger described him the "gayest straight man" on U.S. television during the nine-year run of the show (Tanamor 2009).[8]

As discussed in the introduction, Latinos in entertainment texts often perform stereotyped characters who are hyperemotional, heterosexually promiscuous, flamboyant, clownish, and sexist or "macho" (Béltran 2010; Rodriguez 2008). Nuñez's performance of the comedic straight man, especially in the context of his boss Michael's homophobic, sexist, and racist dialogue, created a limited space of critique—perhaps not of whiteness but of stereotypic representations of Latina/os generally and Latino men specifically. Nuñez's character depicted a socially conscious Latino not afraid to challenge the implicit bigoted assumptions of the other characters. His performance of gay Mexican and Latino identity in *The Office* broke stereotypical comedic narratives and unsettled audience expectations about the character and the familiar Latino type.

Unlike Vergara, who easily performs the Latin look and Latina typecasting, Nuñez breaks with the typical Latino typecast on television. Actors with dark straight hair, much lighter skin, and indigenous or white phenotypic facial features are usually cast to play Latino, usually Mexican, characters. Nuñez's darker skin and black phenotypic appearance are not the Latin look that generally defines representations of Mexican men on television, from Edward James Olmos to Benicio del Toro. Oscar the accountant, costumed in conservative business attire, preferred elite forms of Western culture and retained a skeptical mistrust of the white and heterosexual characters. Although not initially written as a gay man, the producers play with the failed stereotypic expectations—a gay man who is socially conservative, a Latino who is racially black, a Mexican American who prefers elite Western culture.[9] By casting an Afro-Cuban actor to play a U.S. Mexican gay man, the producers unsettle the normative racial typecasting of Latino men in a popular primetime network show.

The contrast between the character development of Gloria and that of Oscar highlights the limitations of post-racial era TV. Rather than playing the straight man (although in the next chapter I discuss how Vergara does at times perform this comedic role), Gloria is portrayed as the Latin/a clown through Vergara's superb use of physical comedy and the stereotyping of Gloria's Colombian identity and sexuality. The producers' development of Gloria as a hypersexual Latina character relies on stereotypically portraying her difference from the other white heterosexual women on the show. For instance, in the episode "Come Fly with Me" (2009), Gloria takes step-granddaughter Alex out to lunch and shopping. The camera work foregrounds the contrasts in costuming and differences between the bodies and the actors. In doing so the visuals undercut Gloria's progressive dialogue regarding female sexual agency and heterosexual womanhood. Gloria's accent and her colorful, tight-fitting dress works against the character's socially conscious script of female sexual agency. The ethnic and racial identity of the actor and character are gendered to produce a stereotypically and socially expected representation of Latina identity. Instead, Vergara's performance of feminist sexual agency highlights the normative whiteness and socially acceptable heteronormative sexuality of the white female characters.

During a time of increased ethnic and racial conflict in the United States, the visual depiction and development of Latina gender, ethnic, and racial difference makes it easier for general audiences to consume the show. For example, despite Vergara's unprecedented visibility and representation of Latin/a American ethnic difference on primetime television, the producers ultimately engage Gloria's character to recuperate normative traditional values of white U.S. heterosexual family life. Within the overall narrative of the series, and as marked in the casting breakdown, Gloria's character is defined by her presumably biologically inherited cultural skills for motherhood and heterosexual marriage. The hipster racism of *Modern Family* celebrates a bygone era, an era when white men were valued as the financial providers of a middle-class life and white women were held up as a model of domesticity.

Post-racial-era TV producers may play with gender and sexual transgressions through the gay married couple, May–December romance, or unruly Latina spitfire characters, but TV's characters and storylines rarely threaten dominant norms of white masculinity or femininity. Indeed, on *Modern Family* most episodes close with a reflection on the continuing importance of the core normative values of white heterosexual middle-class family life. For example, the Christmas episode "Undeck the Halls" (2009), in which tensions arise between Manny, Gloria, and Jay over what cultural traditions to celebrate, concludes with Jay's reflections over a visual montage of the extended family celebrating its intercultural compromise: "Sometimes the best memories are the most untraditional. This is the year the word tradition got a lot bigger." Gloria and Manny's Colombian difference is assimilated into the visual of the Pritchett family's traditional Christmas celebration and the episode's closing through the patriarchal voice of authority and white heteronormative family life. The writers' deployment of the Latina spitfire character and the stereotypic depiction of Gloria illustrate the limitations of multicultural casting in colorblind sitcoms of the post-racial TV era. In other words, the visibility of ethnic and racial minority characters does not translate into more diverse or progressive storylines or characters.

A White Man's Version of *Modern Family*

The progressive possibilities of multicultural casting, colorblind humor, and hipster racism in the post-racial era are connected to the ethnic, racial, and gender structures of television production itself (Molina-Guzmán 2016; Noriega 2000). Like *Scrubs* and *The Office*, *Modern Family* is a program created and produced by established Hollywood men with a track record of television success, cocreators Steven Levitan (*Just Shoot Me* [1997–2003]) and Christopher Lloyd (*The Golden Girls* [1985–92], *Frasier* [1993–2004]). It is their shared experiences of fatherhood that formed the basis of the show: "During a brainstorming session after the cancellation of *Back to You*, Levitan and Lloyd pitched a lot of terrible sitcom ideas, but in the midst of those bad ideas, the two began telling each other stories about their families, and about their children. It was those stories that would later form the basis of *Modern Family*." (Rowles 2014). They brought others into the writers room with whom they had preexisting creative relationships and who could build on their vision of fatherhood. Levitan and Lloyd wanted the writing staff to reflect their own reality as (white heterosexual) fathers. Dan O'Shannon acknowledged at a 2010 Paley Center event that the producers' goal was to write in sexual, ethnic, and racial difference in ways that pushed the comedic desire for innovation and creativity but passed the conservative tendencies of network executives. For the writers, *Modern Family* offered the opportunity to create a unique perspective on contemporary white heteronormative families by testing how far television executives were willing to go on depictions of ethnicity, race, and sexuality.

Both of *Modern Family*'s showrunners and all of the writing staff for *Modern Family*'s first season were white heterosexual men. Showrunner Levitan (169 episodes) and writers Jeffrey Morton, Brad Walsh, and Danny Zuker (168) are listed as the main executive producers (lead writers), along with Chris Smirnoff (148), Abraham Higginbotham (147), and Lloyd (147). In television, the main writers of a particular episode receive production credit. Only two women (Sally Young, credited in 119 episodes, and Elaine Ko, credited in 97 episodes) have received production credits on a program where two of the main characters are women. No Latina/o writers and only one major writer who openly identifies as a gay man, Abraham Higginbotham, who became part of the writers room and received substantial executive production credit, worked on the show. As a result of the lack of women and Latina/o writers, Vergara has talked about the need to ad-lib material: "Yeah! When *Modern Family* was just beginning, I'd have to tell the writers what I thought would be better for me to say. Most of them are American men, so to write for a Latin woman is not as natural for them as writing for Julie [Bowen], for example. Because they have wives like Julie, sisters like Julie, you know what I mean? But now they're so good; they're like hot Latin girls!" (Dunn 2011). When asked by an audience member at the 2010 Paley Center event about the lack of women writers on a show where female characters play such a pivotal role in the narrative, Levitan responded awkwardly: "Yes, we have two right now. They aren't here because they weren't with us all season. And we are really embarrassed here, that we have, especially, all white guys. This year we also added, last year we didn't have any gay writers on the show, we made offers to, now we have two." The two women, Ko and Young, have never received executive production credit, meaning that while they were part of the writers room and performed the role of lead writers, they have never been in charge of the production of a television episode. In addition, telling in Levitan's response to the audience question is that of greater concern was the lack of a gay writer for the show's gay male characters.

While the completely heterosexual, white, and male writing crew for *Modern Family*'s first season is uncomfortable writing for gay characters, they display little discomfort in writing stories for a woman or Latina character. *Modern Family* becomes yet another white heterosexual male production of family life in the United States. Gloria's character is predominantly written through the perspective of the heterosexual white male gaze. She is not a character whose life is meant to speak to the experiences of Latina/o audiences but rather a character who functions as a vehicle for the fantasies, desires, and imaginations of white producers writing for an imagined white middle-class audience. Post-racial-era TV comedy is profoundly constrained by the ethnic, racial, and gender structures of white patriarchal privilege that define production work—even at a moment when the commonsense belief is that the United States has presumably moved beyond race.

READING AGAINST THE POST-RACIAL TV LATINA

APRIL: My mom is Puerto Rican. That is why I'm so lively and colorful.

AUBREY PLAZA ("SISTER CITY" 2010)

GLORIA (speaking to Jay): Years from now, Manny will never remember that a few friends teased him. He'll only remember that his parents support him. That's the most important thing.

SOFÍA VERGARA ("RUN FOR YOUR WIFE" 2009)

Latina/o audiences read and make sense of TV messages about them in complicated and contradictory ways (Báez 2014; Vargas 2009). The previous chapter focused on conservative readings of multicultural casting, colorblind humor, and hipster racism. Specifically, I argued that colorblind humor and hipster racism potentially reinforce stereotypes and biased perceptions of U.S. Latina/os. In this chapter, I read against the post-racial era depictions of ethnicity by recovering the progressive possibilities in Latina visibility. I privilege the questions asked and observations made by Latina/o media scholars, students, and audiences about this work on *Modern Family*. Latina/o audience interpretations are not monolithic, and the emotional responses are neither linear nor direct. Rather, it is possible to experience offense, jeers, tears, and laughter, sometimes at once, to the writers' depiction of Colombian Latina ethnicity.

Since the 1960s U.S. Latina/o actors, cultural producers, and Latina/o audiences have agitated for the right of cultural citizenship, the right to represent ourselves and to be represented with complexity in mainstream media texts (Noriega 2000). As industry studies of Latina/o participation in TV production and content creation document, it is a right that remains elusive. Communications scholar Jillian Báez (2014) observes that Latina audiences smartly negotiate stereotyping and invisibility by recuperating or rejecting the often hypersexualized and heavily commercialized images of Latinas in their readings. As Latina audiences, we actively create spaces of interpretative pleasure in the pieces, snippets, and slices of Latina representations in the mainstream English-language media (Valdivia 2000).

Why Does TV Visibility Matter?

TV, as a representation of the popular and the everyday, cultivates, normalizes, and mainstreams the social segregation and political denigration of Latina/os and other ethnic and racial minorities (Morgan, Shanahan, and Signorelli 2012). Entertainment discourses exist alongside political discourses in the news media, and both contribute to the cognitive process of dehumanization. Neuropsychological communications research finds that dehumanizing visuals and language in the 2016 U.S. presidential campaign influenced the public's perceptions and political support for anti-immigration public policies, such as the border wall with Mexico and the anti-Muslim immigration ban (Kteily and Bruneau 2017). It may be inferred that TV representations of Latina/o difference, like those produced through colorblind humor and hipster racism, also contribute to a political climate that normalizes support for President Trump and his administration's anti-Latina/o policies, like the deportation and separation of undocumented fathers and mothers from their children.

Power is always at play in the cultural politics of mainstream media visibility and erasure. Cultural theorist Stuart Hall (1997) notes, "Power, it seems, has to be understood here, not only in terms of economic exploitation and physical coercion, but also in broader cultural or symbolic terms, including the power to represent someone or something in a certain way—within a certain regime of representation. This includes the exercise of symbolic power through representational practices" (259). For Hall, representations of difference are shaped by the white hetero-patriarchal institutions of media production and anxieties about the loss of institutional power and privilege within these cultural institutions. Highlighting the cracks, slivers, and slippages in TV texts, I reread post-racial era comedic representation of Latinas "to mobilize everything that [cultural studies] can find in terms of intellectual resources in order to understand what keeps making the lives we live and the societies we live in, profoundly and deeply antihuman in their capacity to live with difference" (Hall 1992, 17–18). The representation is important because to be culturally visible is to be socially and politically legible.

Reading the Antiexotic Latina

As discussed in previous chapters, the development of characters like Carla (Reyes) and Oscar (Nuñez) enabled a new Latina/o type—the antiexotic Latina/o—to emerge in post-racial era TV comedy. The antiexotic Latina/o character was usually cast in the role of straight (wo)man in the comedic production of hipster racism, also known as implicit racism, sexism, homophobia. My conservative reading of Vergara's role in *Modern Family* in chapter 2 suggests that the role normalizes hipster racism. A more progressive reading of the antiexotic Latina/o recognizes that the character also functions as a critique of the dominant regime of representation and symbolic reproduction of white heteronormative privilege and power.

Perhaps one of the most interesting examples of the antiexotic Latina role during the post-racial era of TV comedy is the character of April (Aubrey Plaza) in *Parks and Recreation* (see figure 6). Rather than employ the casting of Latina blackness to decenter dominant representations, as was the case for Carla and Oscar, Plaza's character disrupts stereotypic assumptions about the Latina type through her oppositional performance of Latina whiteness. Plaza, who identifies as bisexual, racially white, and of mixed-ethnic Puerto Rican heritage, visually fits the Latina type preferred by Hollywood casting agents. However, even though she can perform the Latina type given her white racial identity, brown eyes, and straight dark hair, Plaza has spent her acting and stand-up career playing against the exotic Latina stereotype through her muted performances of ethnic and sexual identity. Indeed, the creators of *Parks and Recreation* developed the character exclusively for Plaza: "'Aubrey came over to my office and made me feel really uncomfortable for like an hour, and immediately I wanted to put her in the show,' [Michael Schur] has said" (Tsuruoka 2012). Interestingly, the sense of discomfort produced by Plaza is the complete opposite of the culturally comforting role traditionally played by Latin/a American actors and characters, such as the Latin spitfire. The writers deliberately deploy Plaza's nontraditional performance of gender and ethnic identity against TV's dominant Latina stereotypes and typecasting.

Plaza's performance of April as an awkward, shy, underachieving tomboy who eschews the standard expectations of Latina heterosexuality and white femininity is central to progressive readings of the role. She is usually costumed in loose baggy clothes and drab or dark colors (see

Figure 6. Aubrey Plaza / *Parks and Recreation*

figure 7). Although she feigns emotional disinterest in the lives of her coworkers, the character is developed as a loyal, trusted friend and a colleague who struggles with her own emotional and professional insecurities. Plaza's April more often than not performs annoyance, disgust, or an utter lack of interest in the people and events around her. For instance, after Leslie accidentally offends Pawnee voters during her recall election, April returns with her from London to work on small community service projects, such as dealing with Pawnee's slug problem ("London" 2013). April feigns disinterest in Leslie's emotional distress. In one particular scene, she is halfheartedly helping Leslie pick slugs. April maintains her apathetic demeanor and sarcastic tone of voice, becoming "excited" only at the mention of the wolverine-wrangling Mongolian role model she met on the trip: "Yeah, her name was Khongordzol . . . and I love her more than anything in the world." Staring directly into the camera, Plaza delivers her lines in a monotone voice with nonexpressive facial features. Yet, her participation in Leslie's slug project and concern for her friend's morale undercuts Plaza's performance of emotional apathy.

On the surface, the production aesthetics of *Parks and Recreation* and its multicultural ensemble cast appear to mirror *The Office*. Greg Daniels and Michael Schur, who co-executive-produced both shows, developed *Parks and Recreation* in the shadow of *The Office*'s success. Inspired by the events of the 2007 Democratic primary between Obama and Hillary Clinton, the production team decided they wanted Amy Poehler to play lead in an office comedy set in government. Daniels and Schur also decided the tone of the show would mirror the ideological optimism of the 2008 presidential election.

Figure 7. Aubrey Plaza in a yellow hoodie / *Parks and Recreation*

Alan Yang, one of the show's lead writers and coproducer on Aziz Ansari's *Master of None* (Netflix, 2015–Present), described *Parks and Recreation*'s comedic intent:

> One of the great things Mike brought to the show in terms of writing was there could be comedy when characters generally got along and want to do the right thing. A lot of comedy seems negative and built on conflict and that stuff can be really funny, but if you look at some shows, sometimes the characters are just mean to each other. So, one of the challenges of *Parks and Rec*, that I hope we met, was that the characters were friends who had conflicts that were based on personality types and not based on zingers.

Four years after *The Office*'s premiere, *Parks and Recreation*'s storylines and multicultural cast of characters reproduced the colorblind comedy of post-racial era TV. Daniels and Schur built on their formula from *The Office* by hiring a more diverse writers room than the typical TV program. Amy Poehler and Alan Yang both received extensive production credit in the series.[1] However, for the writers of *Parks and Recreation*, the colorblind humor turned away from the caustic comedy of hipster racism toward more feel-good narratives featuring a loveable multicultural cast of characters. The show's writing cleverly played with the stereotypic ethnic and racial expectations of TV audiences in a way similar to *Scrubs*.

Diversity in the writers room plays a significant factor in the comedic writing and character development and also contributes to opening the creative pipeline for writers of color. For example, in *Parks and Recreation*, actor Aziz Ansari, himself a skilled writer, worked with the producers to develop the Americanized Indian American character Tom Haverford (Aziz Ansari) into a loveable metrosexual with impeccable fashion style and a keen business sense, a unique second-generation Indian American character. Likewise, Retta's character, the wealthy, tech-savvy, classically trained singer Donna Meagle, counters dominant media stereotypes about African American women as urban, poor, and lacking cultural capital. The casting of a dark-skinned and heavyset actor in the role defied casting expectations for African American women on TV and film, expectations that often reward black women actors who meet Western standards of feminine beauty such as Halle Berry or Kerry Washington. Retta, as an actor, does not physically meet the casting norms of TV beauty and sexuality, yet the writers develop the character to be one of the most sexually attractive and desired on the show.

Rather than engage hipster racism to produce humor, the comedy on *Parks and Recreation* relies on writing that plays against standard typecasting, employs in-depth character development, and produces storylines that play against ethnic, racial, and gender stereotypes. The colorblind values in the show make use of audiences' preexisting knowledge of ethnic and racial stereotypes to produce laughter. And the show's critique of ethnic and racial stereotypes depends on developing complex ethnic and racial characters. Thus, like *Scrubs*, it is possible for some post-racial era comedies to reinforce colorblindness but avoid hipster racism and standard TV conventions regarding the typecasting and stereotyping of ethnic and racial minority characters.

Parks and Recreation, for instance, trends away from hipster racism by producing an ironic twist on what Kristen Warner (2015) terms color consciousness, such as the development of the comedy around April's Puerto Rican ethnicity. April's ethnicity is not worked into the narrative until the fifth episode of the second season, and when it is referenced it is done in a manner as subdued as the character herself

("Sister City" 2009). Leslie, who is monolingual, anxiously recruits April to serve as interpreter for a meet and greet with Pawnee's sister-city colleagues from Nicaragua. After the meeting, April, who is costumed in loose-fitting, neutral-colored clothes, gives a sarcastic on-camera interview in heavily accented Spanish: "My mom is Puerto Rican. That is why I'm so lively and colorful." Audiences are positioned to laugh at the writers' critique of Latina media stereotypes and of stereotypic assumptions that all Latina/os speak Spanish, are hyper-emotional, and wear colorful clothing. The episode further pokes fun at the monolingual limitations of most U.S. citizens and audiences by setting up a contrast between the Nicaraguan's delegation, which is fluent in English, and the Pawnee team, which only speaks English, except April, sort of. Thus, the producers develop the ethnicity of April's character, much like they do for the other ethnic and racial minorities on the show, by relying on humor that disrupts audiences' expectations and familiarity with ethnic and racial TV stereotypes. In this instance, the absence of a laugh track invites audiences to laugh at the producers' smart take on the ethnocentric assumptions of the characters and mainstream white U.S. audiences.

Although *Modern Family* and *Parks and Recreation* premiered in the same year, Plaza's acting and character are the binary opposite of Vergara's depiction of Gloria. Plaza's character is the antithesis of the Latina spitfire. Although in later seasons April's costuming and makeup become more normatively feminized, the producers never sexualize her. For instance, when April marries her boyfriend Andy (Chris Pratt) at an informal, impromptu wedding party ("Andy and April's Fancy Party" 2011), the writers avoid standard television conventions of heterosexual weddings. Other than the episode's mellow and sentimental soundtrack for the wedding ceremony, nothing else in the production follows television norms. April's gay ex-boyfriend is cast as one of the flower girls. His boyfriend is cast as the other flower girl. The vows include lines such as this one, delivered in typical deadpan Plaza fashion: "I guess I hate most things but I never seem to hate you. So, I wanna spend the rest of my life with you. Is that cool?" Emphasizing the writer's decision to work against generic TV and stereotypic expectations of heterosexuality and Latina femininity, the post-wedding celebration begins with the accidental release of a dead pigeon by the show's famously incompetent marijuana-smoking animal control staff (Harris Wittels and Colton Dunn). The specificity of April's mixed Puerto Rican identity is part of the comic background rather than the narrative foreground. In other words, it informs the comedy surrounding April, but it does not drive April's storylines or character development. Perhaps the smart and progressive quality of the humor is the reason *Parks and Recreation* had a shorter and less successful run than either *The Office* or *Modern Family*.

The Exotic Latina Straight Man

Colorblind comedy, hipster racism, and comedic performances by Latina/o actors complicate the culture of Latina/o invisibility and stereotyping on film, news, and primetime TV. For instance, Vergara, Gloria, and *Modern Family* are ubiquitous, appearing in U.S. homes, laptops, and smartphones. Vergara's visibility occurs alongside legislative efforts to restrict and penalize Latina/o immigration across the United States. Her performance as Gloria is increasingly a beloved and iconic part of the U.S. cultural landscape during a historical moment when Latin American immigrants and, by implication, U.S. Latina/os are politically represented as a threat to the economic and domestic security of the nation. So even as the writers of *Modern Family* invite audiences to laugh at or with dialogue grounded in hipster racism and Vergara's spitfire performance, her portrayal of Gloria as the comedic straight man also reminds audiences that U.S. Latina/os and their lives are nuanced and complex.

In the context of intensified U.S. racial and ethnic antagonisms, rereading Gloria through a progressive frame requires audiences to engage in what Angharad Valdivia (2000) conceptualizes as the "theory of frustration," a reading practice developed by Latina audiences as a response to media in/visibility and stereotyping. A frustrated reading of *Modern Family*'s Gloria provides Latina/o audiences a unique opportunity to laugh at ourselves, to see ourselves in mainstream cultural texts, even as we sometimes cringe at the dialogue and plotlines. It is not surprising that despite the hipster racism embedded in the show's scripts, it is a top-ten-rated show for U.S. Latina/o audiences (Nielsen Company 2014). Latina/o laughter thus disrupts hipster racism and the colorblind invisibility of ethnicity and race on TV screens, even as ethnic and racial inequities continued unabated in the world outside TV.

As discussed in the previous chapter, Vergara meets the ideals of advertisers and expectations of audiences for Latina typecasting (ambiguously white, physically curvaceous, linguistically accented) and for developing TV characters based on familiar Latina stereotypes. The writing also carves out spaces for more progressive audience readings by using Vergara's role as comedic straight man to draw attention to the white privilege of the characters and, consequently, the normalization of whiteness in the program. The double-sided nature of Gloria's character development and storylines is due, in part, to the different comedic approaches of the executive producers. Entertainment blogger Dustin Rowles describes the split: "Lloyd preferred the classier brand of comedy he'd perfected in *Frasier*, while Levitan veered toward the kind of comedy you'd expect from a sitcom starring Pamela Anderson called *Stacked*" (Rowles 2014).[2] Scripted moments of seriousness or sentimentality create openings for a more compelling version of gendered ethnic difference in post-racial era TV. Similar to the role of April in *Parks and Recreation*, *Modern Family*'s depiction of Gloria produces frustrated readings of visibility and social critique.

The combination of hipster racism and the color-conscious critique of white heteronormative privilege and the post-racial discourse that sustains it produces a more three-dimensional Latina character. In *Modern Family*, for example, Vergara performs both the sexualized Latina clown—mispronouncing words, making grammatical errors, yelling in Spanish, and rolling her R's—and the less stereotypical Latina straight man. In particular, Vergara's straight-man performance counterbalances the comedy of hipster racism by explicitly and implicitly highlighting the racist, xenophobic, or socially inappropriate actions and dialogue of the white characters. Vergara's performance of the straight man produces teachable moments critical of the contemporary ethnic and racial climate. To do so *Modern Family*'s writers soften the spitfire stereotype by developing Vergara's more humorous and sympathetic performance of undocumented Latina identity and immigrant motherhood. The Lloyd-esque writing creates a more emotionally complicated character and compelling depiction of Latinas, one palatable to a broader audience.

Representing Latina Motherhood in the U.S. Media

Cultural ideas about motherhood are central to U.S. storytelling about Latinas in the media. It is also one of the dominant tropes through which the media genders Latinidad. The self-sacrificing, almost virginal Latina mother is a staple of Hollywood dramas about Latina/os, specifically in representations of Mexican women. The opposite tends to be true of Latina motherhood in comedies. For instance, in television comedies or dramatic comedies (dramadies), Latina motherhood is sometimes depicted through over-the-top narratives of self-sacrifice. And that motherly sacrifice is sometimes associated with religiously moral and conservative stereotypes about Catholicism and female sexuality, as seen in the title character Jane (Gina Rodriguez) in *Jane the Virgin* or Amy in *Superstore*. However, most often Latina mothers in primetime comedies are portrayed as working-class, hyperfeminine, sexual, and sexually desirable, as is the case with Gloria in *Modern Family*, Xiomara (Andrea Navedo) in *Jane the Virgin*, and Hilda (Ana Ortiz) in *Ugly Betty*, among other examples.

Fictional constructions of Latina motherhood on entertainment TV exist alongside a contrasting set of news discourses of Latina motherhood. Until the Trump administration's hardline enforcement of anti-immigration policies in 2017, mainstream news stories featuring self-sacrificing Latin/a American mothers were rare with only a few exceptions—coverage of deceased Cuban refugee Elisabet Brotons, the ensuing international custody battle over Elián Gonzalez, and the deportation of sanctuary activist Elvira Arellano away from her U.S.-born son Saul Arellano (Cacho 2012; Molina-Guzmán 2010). For the most part, journalistic framing of Latinas and Latin/a American women focus on criminality, hyperfertility, and foreignness (Amaya 2013; Chavez 2001; Santa Ana 2002). English-language news tends to gender immigration issues by foregrounding the significance of Latina motherhood to the institution of Latina/o families, whereas ethnic media coverage genders immigration by humanizing the issue with stories of familial and motherly sacrifice (Molina-Guzmán 2010). More recent news coverage of Latin American immigration in the English-language news also frames Latin/a American mothers as criminally negligent and children as criminals.

Historically, mainstream media depictions of Latina/o immigration, motherhood, and families have also varied significantly across the three largest U.S. Latina/o ethnic groups: Cubans, Puerto Ricans, and Mexicans. Until the 1980s, news media discourses about Cubans and Cuban migration reinforced notions of Cuban exceptionalism and U.S. Cold War foreign policy. Throughout the 1960s and 1970s, Cuban exiles were specifically constructed in the news, films, and television programs as white, educated, politically conservative, and ideologically committed to U.S. capitalism and democracy, as in the PBS show *¿Que Pasa, USA?* (1977–80). For example, U.S. news coverage of the 1960s "Pedro Pan" program, which allowed parents opposed to Cuba's communist government to send their unaccompanied children to the United States, garnered sympathetic coverage (Torres 2004). News images of these young children leaving their weeping mothers and families in Cuba and entering the United States alone encouraged empathy toward Cuban families and mothers as political refugees rather than ethnic immigrants (Torres 2004). The emotionally laden visuals of motherless child refugees arriving in the United States symbolized the repressive consequences of communism and allowed popular Cold War rhetoric to work as a type of propaganda for U.S. political goals.

In contrast, the hundreds of thousands of Mexican and Puerto Rican laborers who came to the United States under the Bracero Program (1948–68) and Operation Bootstrap (1950s), respectively, faced political, economic, racial, and linguistic discrimination as well as negative media representations (Arredondo 2008; Fernández 2012; Loza 2016; Whalen and Vázquez-Hernández 2008). The United States provided exiled Cubans with special financial and educational programs to assist their transition while denying Mexicans and Puerto Ricans working in labor-intensive agricultural, manufacturing, and domestic service jobs access to federal assistance or legal protection. Braceros toiled mostly under environmentally substandard working conditions in the agricultural fields of California, the Southwest, and the Midwest, and Puerto Ricans, especially women, were primarily expected to work in low-wage nonunion manufacturing and domestic service jobs in the Northeast and Midwest. While Cubans and Puerto Ricans were encouraged to come to the United States as heteronormative family units, male Bracero workers were often forced to leave their families behind in Mexico. News and entertainment coverage overwhelmingly depicted Puerto Rican and Mexican immigrants as unclean, uneducated, poor, and racially not white.

Because Cubans were welcomed as political refugees whose presence within the nation would be temporary, they benefited from mostly benign media depictions devoid of negative ethnic and racial stereotypes. On the other end of the representational spectrum, Spanish Caribbean, Mexican, and other Latin American immigrants remain mired in racialized depictions of these communities as economic migrants—not racially white and negatively coded as poor, uneducated, aberrantly fertile, and undeserving of public sympathy or legal protection. As a point of contrast to Cuban representations, Puerto Rican migrants, who are born U.S. citizens, are usually depicted in the media as poor, uneducated, sexually fertile, exotic, and racially black (Rodríguez 1989, 1997). Both Puerto Ricans and Mexicans have faced negative media representations, particularly during moments of economic crisis such as the Great Depression and the Great Recession.

The Central American refugee crisis of 2014 brought to the media foreground the plight of women and children escaping social, political, and economic turmoil (Menjívar 2014, 2016). According to the Pew Research Center (Motel and Patten 2012), aside from Mexico, immigrants from El Salvador, Guatemala, and Honduras represent the largest segment of undocumented populations entering the United States. The causes of Central American immigration are complicated. Beginning in the 1850s, U.S. foreign policy in Central America has supported brutal military regimes to protect military and economic interests (Menjívar 2011). Funding from the U.S. War on Drugs and more recently post–September 11th anti-terror programs have enabled the continuation of government-backed military campaigns against mostly indigenous, rural, and working-class communities.

The increasing use of gendered violence by military and guerilla groups remains a major factor in the growing number of Central American women and child immigrants seeking asylum in the United States (Menjívar 2011; Menjívar and Abrego 2012; Menjívar and Lakhani 2016). Ironically, women immigrants from El Salvador, Guatemala, and Honduras, all countries considered to be democracies and economically and politically friendly to the United States, face a more difficult path to refugee status than, for example, immigrants from Cuba (Salcido and Menjívar 2012; Oboler 2006). Labeling immigrants from these countries as political refugees enables them to ask for political asylum and calls into question the military involvement of the United States in supporting these governments (Menjívar 2011). The contemporary political backlash toward and mainstream news coverage of Central American women and child refugees draw further attention to the differences in the media depiction of Latina/o and Latin American communities. While Cuba's Pedro Pan generation was greeted with sympathy and public resources, Central American refugees are defined by journalistic images and narratives that raise questions about their claims to refugee status.

Colombian immigrants are relatively absent from media depictions—with the exception of television and film portrayals of the violence surrounding Colombian drug cartels, such as *Blow* (2001) and *Colombiana* (2011) (Cepeda 2010). The long-lasting Colombian conflict has resulted in almost 250,000 deaths as well as decades of human rights violations, including children being forced into military service by socialist rebels. Yet, the percentage of Colombian immigrants living in the United States, which peaked in the 1970s and 1980s at the height of the U.S.-backed war with socialist rebels, remains small at 1.9 percent (Motel and Patten 2012). Like other Central American refugees, Colombian immigrants face a difficult path to refugee or legal migration status in the United States. And today U.S. citizens of Colombian descent make up only a small percentage of the Latina/o population. This background on the entertainment and news coverage of Latina American immigration is provided to contextualize the performance by Vergara on *Modern Family*. In particular, the following section examines how Vergara, who is a wealthy Colombian woman, and her depiction of Gloria, a wealthy Colombian immigrant, introduces a more progressive politics of visibility.

Giving Face to Undocumented Immigrants

The lack of media attention to the Colombian military conflict and the general invisibility of Colombian communities within news coverage of undocumented Latina/o immigration to the United States made the decision to cast Vergara a safer choice for developing an undocumented Latina character for primetime comedic television.

Given the above context of media stereotypes about Latina mother-hood and Latin/a American immigration, Gloria and her onscreen son Manny (Rico Rodriguez) produce an interesting space of cultural visibility for Latina/o audiences.

For example, references to Gloria and Manny's past in Colombia create a funny and sympathetic immigration narrative for the characters, such as in this scene from the first-season episode "Run for Your Wife" (see figure 8):

> *Jay joins Gloria at Manny's classroom.*
> GLORIA: Years from now, Manny will never remember that a few friends teased him, he'll only remember that his parents support him. That's the most important thing.
> *Manny comes out to join them.*
> MANNY: Is something wrong? Who has died?
> GLORIA: No one, Manny.
> JAY: Why would you even think that?
> GLORIA: In Colombia, Manny went to Pablo Escobar Elementary School. If you got pulled out of class, it was to identify a body.

Figure 8. Sofía Vergara and blue lockers

Gloria's punch line draws out the contrast between the character's immigrant background and the white family. The scene's visuals of Manny dressed in a poncho do reproduce hipster racism as Manny's outfit is positioned as the joke. Gloria's reference to the drug-fueled and military violence in which many Colombian children have grown up further reinforces Gloria and Manny's sense of foreignness. As frustrating as these stereotypical depictions might be, it is also lines like "he'll only remember that his parents support him" that have earned the show a respectable Latina/o audience. With regard to their depiction of Latina motherhood, the writers develop a character defined by her social acceptance of gender, sexual, ethnic, and racial diversity as well as her unconditional love for her sons and family. Vergara's performance of motherhood pushes against dominant Latina stereotypes. Delivering dialogue with sincere compassion, Vergara provides the character with an emotional depth that complicates the spitfire stereotype upon which the character is modeled.

Additionally, the scene highlights the producers' decision to develop Manny as the antiexotic straight man, a decision that further disrupts media stereotypes of Latino youth as urban, uneducated, and poor. On the show, Rodriguez, whose character was age ten at the start of the show, performs a highly educated and emotionally mature role that contrast with both the hyperemotional Gloria and the less intellectually savvy Jay. In doing so, Rodriguez plays against the hypermasculine Latino stereotype prevalent on film and television. In comparison to the casting of Vergara, who has a pronounced Spanish accent, the producers requested that Rodriguez take diction lessons to remove all traces of an accent from his performance of Manny.

Ethnic-specific identity and experiences are sometimes central to adding dimension to the characters and storylines in post-racial comedies. In *Modern Family*, for example, Vergara's Colombian identity allows the producers to create a stereotypic Latina character without the racial legacy surrounding Mexican and Puerto Rican characters on TV. Because Colombians are rarely depicted on TV and rarely linked with undocumented immigration or negative news coverage of Central American immigration, *Modern Family*'s producers create an undocumented immigrant character without the racially charged associations of Mexican border crossers. Casting Vergara and Manny as Colombian immigrants racially depoliticizes the show and enables the primetime television show to feature an undocumented immigrant Latina character in a starring ensemble role. Indeed, Gloria's identity as an undocumented immigrant is a running joke on the show, and the character does not become a U.S. citizen until the sixth season ("Patriot Games" 2015).

Gloria's Colombian identity and citizenship status allow the writers to develop a comedic critique of white upper-middle-class identity and privilege. By drawing attention to a more performance-based reading of Gloria's character, I am not minimizing the troubling observations made in previous chapters. The writing staff does employ Gloria's character to produce colorblind humor and hipster racism. Negative references and jokes about Colombians, Latinas, and "illegal aliens" in relation to Gloria's character abound throughout the series. And depicting a Colombian or Latina/o immigrant without legal U.S. documentation of citizenship is not, in and of itself, funny. In fact, as news reports of Trump's anti-immigrant policies illustrate, being an undocumented Latina/o, Asian, African, or Arab immigrant remains quite dangerous.

However, Vergara's more nuanced performance of Gloria equally serves as a narrative and visual counterpoint to hipster racism, journalistic coverage, and political rhetoric about undocumented Central American/Mexican immigrants, a rhetoric that since the 1800s has defined Mexican and Latin American migration as a threatening mass of unruly brown bodies (Amaya 2013; Ono and Sloop 2002; Santa Ana 2002). The development and performance of Gloria's character as a compassionate, intelligent, and fiercely devoted mother to her firstborn son (and her son with Jay) clashes with news and entertainment stereotypes of U.S. Latinas and Latin/a American women as sexually permissive, uneducated, and criminal. In particular, the birth of Fulgencio Joseph, or Joe (Rebecca and Sierra Mark, Pierce Wallace, Jeremy Maguire), into the Pritchett family household enhances the emotional texture of Gloria's character. For example, Joe's birth in season four ("Party Crasher" 2013) and his subsequent baptism ("Fulgencio" 2013) allowed the writers to bring Gloria's mother, Pilar (Elizabeth Peña), and sister, Sonia (Stephanie Beatriz), from Colombia to Los Angeles and into the narrative. Their presence in the storylines highlight Gloria's ethnic difference through the development of key elements of Gloria's background story and romance between Gloria and Jay. With the birth of Joe, whose nickname is an intercultural compromise between Jay and Gloria, the writing foregrounds her role as sister and daughter and emphasize the fraught negotiations and intercultural conflicts between Gloria and her family. Post-Joe storylines have also focused on the maternal, spousal, and sexual insecurities arising from the birth of a new child. The development of Gloria beyond the spitfire stereotype and toward an emotionally complex mother figure contributes to the feel-good nature of the show and, perhaps unintentionally, provides a compassionate contrast to the news images and stories about U.S. Latina/o and Latin American criminality.

Producing a program for the consumption of a predominantly white and wealthy audience demands the creation of novel characters depicted in culturally safe and familiar ways for TV executives and audiences. So, it perhaps takes a writing crew of privileged white men to make fun of undocumented immigrants and to create a beloved undocumented Latina character. In *Modern Family*, for instance, Gloria's role as a stay-at-home mother enables audience readings of the character as a socially conservative and respectable heteronormative woman. Gloria's age, undocumented status, and ethnic identity also creates opportunities for other audiences to take pleasure in the critique of white privilege the character provides. The following scene, which occurs after Gloria learns that Claire called her a gold digger, presents an example of this dualistic reading ("Coal Digger" 2009):

> GLORIA: Okay. Just let me ask you one thing, and it's okay if the answer is no. Are you happy I married your father?
>
> CLAIRE: Happy?
>
> GLORIA *(a little bothered)*: I knew it.
>
> CLAIRE: I'm still getting used to it, that's all. You don't expect to wake up one day with a new mom that looks like she fell off a tool calendar. But I'm happy you make him happy, which you do, in many ways—*(points to the lingerie in the room)*—and many colors.
>
> GLORIA: And he makes me happy, too. And not just with money. He's good to Manny, he's got a good heart, he's a wonderful lover—
>
> CLAIRE: Okay . . .

The storyline in this episode revolves around the characters' stereotypic responses to Gloria's age, ethnicity, and performance of sexuality (the lingerie in different colors, the comments on Jay's sexual skills). By focusing on Claire's discomfort with Gloria, the episode and scene allow the writers to subtly call out the prejudices of the white characters. Speaking about the character of Gloria at a 2010 Paley Center event, Levitan suggested: "And the key to Gloria is that she is not a bimbo and she's not a gold-digger, a coal digger. That she is fiercely protective of Manny and she's strong. And Jay thought that he had married, his old wife was a pain in the ass and he got divorced, and he thought he had married the hot young thing that was going to make his life really sweet and easy and he stepped into it again. Even worse. Tougher than the first one. That is sort of the character." Another writer, Dan O'Shannon, added that audiences' (and network executives') acceptance of the character is also dependent on the producers' decision not to depict the sexual relationship. Yet, the writers' development of the character and Vergara's sympathetic performance produce a frustrated interpretative space of Latina visibility in the context of xenophobic anti-immigrant discourses and policies in the United States.

Throughout *Modern Family*'s run the writing team engages Gloria to produce an implicit critique of whiteness. Using wordplay with terms like "alien," this line from Jay's dialogue with Manny about his biological father illustrates the point ("The Bicycle Thief" 2009): "The only way he's like Superman is that they both landed in this country illegally." Because there is no visual or verbal response, Jay's pejorative use of the term "illegal" is left explicitly uncontested. At the same time, the writers' comparison of an undocumented Colombian immigrant to an icon of white male masculinity, Superman, comically communicates the absurdity of the term "illegal alien" by drawing attention to the ways whiteness protects some nonethnic immigrants from the anti-immigrant slur. Similar to other scenes where Gloria's former citizenship status is used to create humor, the comedy in the above exchange creates a critique of the racial power of language.

The writing of other ethnic characters on the show works in similar ways. For example, Mitchell and Cameron's interaction with an assimilated Asian pediatrician, Dr. Miura (Suzy Nakayama), is set up as a comic foil to the white couple's desire to be culturally sensitive for their daughter, Lily ("Run for Your Wife" 2009):

> CAMERON: By the way, you'll be pleased to know that Mitchell and I intend to raise Lily with influences from her Asian heritage.
> *Dr. Miura couldn't care less.*

DR. MIURA: That's uh . . . great. Has there been any vomiting since the head bump?
CAMERON: No. *(then)* We've hung some Asian art in her bedroom. And, when she's ready for solid food, there is a great little pho place close to our house. (pronounced "fuh") Am I saying that right? Pho. It's a soup.
DR. MIURA: I don't know. I'm from Denver. We don't have a lot of pho there.

Building on post-racial conservative critiques of the social excesses of multiculturalism and cultural sensitivity, the writers tap into a Trump-like resentment of political correctness in the scene. The producers' use of colorblindness (Dr. Miura's refusal or inability to recognize that she is being read ethnically by Cameron and Mitchell) also brings into question the characters' own privilege and ethnic assumptions.

Troubling Whiteness

Ethnicity, race, and sexual identity are always in the framework of post racial era comedies, thereby implicitly troubling the racism and racial privilege of the white characters. In *Modern Family*, the following three first-season episodes set the pattern for the subtle use of social critique in the series: "The Incident" (2010), "Not in My House" (2010), and "Starry Night" (2010). One storyline in each episode centers on Gloria and her ethnic identity in relation to the family's white privilege. In the previous chapter, I discussed the episode "The Incident," which centered on Jay's ex-wife Dede and her racist behavior at his wedding to Gloria, a recurring behavior throughout the series. For the final section of this chapter, I look at the remaining two episodes to explore the implicit critique of whiteness in post-racial era comedies.

In the series, Cameron and Mitchell are depicted as the most socially progressive couple and sometimes the least socially conscious. For example, in the fourth season the couple panics when Lily claims to Gloria that she is gay, and the couple's ensuing actions end up offending a lesbian couple ("The Future Dunphys" 2013). And in the eighth season, the couple confronts their gender prejudice when they make fun of Tom, Lily's transgender friend played by transgender actor Jackson Millarker ("A Stereotypical Day" 2016). Similarly, the first-season storylines in "Not in My House" (2010) and "Starry Night" (2010) revolve around the couple's misguided and exaggerated attempts at racial sensitivity.

In setting up Vergara as the straight man in relation to Cameron and Mitchell, the characters are reduced to queer clowns, a depiction that has drawn the ire of some gay media activists. "Not in My House" pits Cameron and Mitchell against each other as the couple deals with their despondent Spanish-speaking gardener. Leaving aside the characters' practice of hiring immigrant labor throughout the series, Cameron and Mitchell's visible discomfort with the emotional state of their domestic laborer is the source of comedy. That is to say, the characters' failure to respond to the gardener in a culturally sensitive manner is the object of laughter. In contrast to Cameron and Mitchell, Gloria's bilingual ability is employed in the episode to resolve the narrative conflict. The writers position Vergara's ethnic heterosexual character as linguistically and culturally superior to the white gay couple. Always the wise and loving mother in the series—a common gender stereotype used for developing black and Latina characters on sitcoms—Vergara performs the role of intercultural translator and moral center by pushing the white characters to move beyond ethnic and racial prejudices. Lest the episode become too politically progressive, all the Latina/o characters except Gloria are unnamed, emphasizing their overall insignificance to the storyline. The episode concludes with the following matter-of-fact exchange between Mitchell and his father: "Because of him [Cameron], I have a house full of Latinos." Jay responds, "Welcome to my world." O'Neill's sarcastic delivery emphasizes the white characters' discomfort at sharing a domestic space with Latina/os, even the ones who are part of your family. While Jay as the patriarch of the show is never depicted as racially or sexually progressive—indeed, his nickname for his Vietnamese granddaughter, Lily, is "Fortune Cookie"—the gay couple's racial and ethnic attempts to be culturally sensitive are routinely called into question.

Critiquing whiteness through the performance of queerness rather than white heterosexual masculinity is narratively safer. Indeed, focusing on the ethnic and racial ignorance of the queer characters positions the show as a comic "equal-opportunity offender." One of the central storylines in "Starry Night," for example, arises when Cameron believes he inadvertently offends Gloria at a family party. At the party, Cameron is depicted as uncomfortable around Gloria because he is insecure about her attitude toward gay people. The humor in the scene is partially a play with stereotypic assumptions about Latina/o cultures as heterosexist and homophobic. Cameron attempts to overcome his discomfort by inviting Gloria out to dinner. His plan to eat at an exclusive restaurant is ruined, and instead Gloria invites Cameron to her favorite restaurant in a working-class Colombian neighborhood of Los Angeles where she lived after her divorce. Throughout the episode Stonestreet's performance of Cameron is socially awkward, anxious, and eager to please. Vergara's performance of Gloria is socially comfortable, relaxed, and understated as she wistfully reminisces about her days as an economically struggling and divorced single mother. Her comfortable and relaxed performance stands in contrast to the anxious performance of Stonestreet, who finds himself in a social space foreign to him. The producers visually juxtapose Cameron's behavior against Gloria's social ease. Eventually, the conflict is resolved when Gloria confesses to Cameron that she misses spending time with gay men. Vergara's performance and Gloria's confession play against the prejudiced assumptions that underlie the gay character. Gloria's comfort with and desire for queer company adds complexity to Vergara's performance of the spitfire, an archetype generally defined through its feminized heterosexuality.

Ironically, the critiques of whiteness and white racism, like others in post-racial era comedies, often occur through the bodies and lives of white gay characters, who are often depicted as socially flawed. Vergara's character is developed by the producers as more complex and socially progressive than Cameron. She comfortably moves between different cultural and social spaces—the white middle-class world she inhabits on the series and the working-class immigrant space she once lived in—in ways the white characters cannot. Thus, the writing and Vergara's performance transform the Latina spitfire, allowing audiences a comedic opportunity to reflect on racialized assumptions about Latina/os while also enabling moments of humorous and complex visibility for Latina/o audiences.

As an undocumented Colombian immigrant who leaves an emotionally abusive marriage to stake out a better life for her son, the character's life experiences become comedic foil and critique to the racial and class privilege of the white characters. Whatever disasters or conflicts the other couples face, the producers often write into the episode far more serious experiences from Gloria's past, such as being pulled out of class to identify dead bodies. To some ears the absurdity of this comment might sound funny or even reinforce stereotypic assumptions about Latin America as a violent space. But to some U.S. audiences, specifically Colombians and other Latina/os, it may be recognized as a tragically funny truth. The impact of Latin America's long-running, low-intensity wars on generations of families, women, and children has been massive. Gloria's more violent past in Colombia and history of poverty as an undocumented resident in the United States is set up as a sobering contrast to the "pampered" lives of the other white, affluent family members (except for Cameron, who grew up on a farm in the rural Midwest).

The white characters are rarely as racially conscious as they assume themselves to be compared to the more progressive values of the ethnic working-class immigrant Gloria. Claire is privileged and satirized in the series as the idealized middle-class mother. However, it is the folksy, wise, and naturally nurturing Gloria who often solves the family's dilemmas through the use of "ethnic commonsense." Weaving together nostalgic memories and harrowing experiences of Gloria's past, the writers create an emotionally compelling picture of a difficult immigrant past and a multidimensional ethnic character. In turn, the character's complexity affords Vergara the opportunity to perform a modern take on a classic Latin/a American archetype. Vergara's performance reminds audiences that Latina/o lives are more compelling and diverse than the images depicted on TV or in the news. Her sophisticated performance produces unprecedented visibility and a humorous space of social critique in the context of continuing economic angst, racial backlash, and the meritocratic policies of a post-race neoliberal state.

Vergara as Gloria is popular and socially acceptable to mainstream audiences because of her hypersexualized, always foreign, and at times cartoonish performance of gendered ethnic identity. Yet, any Latina visibility in the context of political hostility toward Latinos and entrenched media invisibility also presents a space to create novel narratives about gender, race, and ethnicity. Vergara's complex performance of the Latina spitfire, of a fiercely protective undocumented single mother, creates a potentially transformative moment of interpretative frustration in the post-racial era of TV.

CONCLUSION

Post-Racial Past and Colorblind Futures on TV

The Joys of Basic Television.

MEGAN GARBER

It is not accidental that in in all but one of the shows discussed here (*The Office*), the primary Latina/o characters are women. For example, Fox's *Brooklyn Nine-Nine* (2013–Present) costars two Latin/a American actors—Melissa Fumero, who is U.S. born of Cuban descent, and Stephanie Beatriz, who is Argentinian.[1] Critically acclaimed Gina Rodriguez in the title role of the less watched *Jane the Virgin* (2014–Present) leads the way for the CW. In 2015, NBC, the network that once led the TV diversity race with shows like *The Cosby Show*, *Scrubs*, and *The Office*, premiered America Ferrera's *Superstore* (2015–Present) and Eva Longoria's *Telenovela* (2015–16). NBC's late entry into Latina/o "diverse programming" led at least one television critic to observe that NBC "finally (got) the diversity memo" (Saraiya 2015). In this concluding chapter, I reflect on what "basic television" looks like in the context of the socially and politically fraught Trump era (2015–Present). Specifically, I reflect on transformations in TV comedic narratives, characters, and styles of humor as commonsense post-racial attitudes and beliefs have been increasingly contested by images of ethnic and racial violence and inequality in the news.

Why Latinas (and Not Latinos) on TV Comedies

Latina/o TV characters tend to be women for several reasons. First, Latina actors and characters are a less threatening way to achieve the network's contemporary diversity goals. Second, Latinas have historically played the role of intercultural interlocutor in U.S. popular culture. In her edited collection, Myra Mendible (2007) summarizes the binary representational history surrounding Latina and

Latin American actors: "Since the early nineteenth century, [Latinas'] racially marked sexuality signaled a threat to the body politic, a foreign other against whom the ideals of the domestic self, particularly its narratives of white femininity and moral virtue, could be defined. At the same time, the Latina body offered a tempting alter/narrative: an exotic object of imperial and sexual desire" (8). The bodies of women, specifically racially ambiguous but ethnically marked U.S.-born and immigrant women, are central to imagining what it means to be "American" and who belongs in the United States. Latin/a American actors and characters are depicted as exotic and sexually desirable, yet they are perceived as less powerful and thereby socially subservient (Molina-Guzmán 2010). The commercial abilities of Latinas, Asian, black, and multiracial women, especially those who can perform a socially acceptable femininity and normative sexuality, offer an effective strategy for creating the appearance of more ethnically and racially inclusive programming. Diversity on screen does not equal Latina diversity behind the camera.

U.S. post-racial era programming depends on ethnic women, specifically Latinas, as the preferred bodies to perform cultural labor, to entertain, and to sell difference to advertisers and audiences. In contemporary media economics, racially ambiguous ethnic women's bodies are easier to market for mainstream audiences and are a more desirable commodity for advertisers. According to the Pew Research Center, six in ten Latina/os are millennial or younger in the United States (Patten 2016). Millennial Latina/os are more likely to be U.S. born and English dominant (Patten 2016). In 2010 Latinas emerged as the largest ethnic and racial minority group among women at 15.9 percent (U.S. Census, 2011). These demographic changes make Latinas one of the largest and youngest groups of consumers in the United States and a central focus of media industry efforts to diversify audiences. With U.S. Latina/os having an estimated $1.4 trillion in buying power, Latinas are a major target for the advertising revenue upon which the networks depend (Advertising Age 2015).

But it is not just any Latina body, as discussed in the introduction, that is marketable to mainstream audiences, but a particular type of Latina body. Ferrera, Longoria, Plaza, and Vergara fit the Latina television type sought by media producers—dark hair, dark eyes, and ambiguously ethnic. Although these actors conform to the physical stereotype of Latinas as curvaceous, feminine, and hetero-sexual, the casting of actors like Ferrera, Plaza, Reyes, Rodriguez, and others also challenge audience expectations about the roles Latinas play on primetime television. For example, similar to Plaza's perfor-mance of Latina identity in *Parks and Recreation*, Ferrera's roles in *Ugly Betty* and in *Superstore* center on characters whose bodies are not the sexualized visual focus of the show and whose sexuality is not the driver of the narrative. Indeed, Ferrera is known for playing Latina TV and film characters depicted as having bodies outside the thin and curvaceous Hollywood norm.

Regardless, Latina characters on comedies generally conform to mainstream television audience expectations of Latina actors as racially white and ethnically ambiguous. The casting privilege given to these actors because they effectively fit the Latina type makes Ferrera and Longoria's 2015 critique of television's typecasting practices par-ticularly ironic (Moreno 2016).[2] Ultimately, as observed by a *New York Times* reviewer, "Two new shows on NBC that address the short-age of Hispanic characters on television play the demographic game about as safely as it can be played, putting well-known Latina stars in nonthreatening, nonchallenging comedies" (Genzlinger 2016). By hiring familiar and popular actors who fit the Latina typecast even as the actors work against Latina stereotypes, network executives, pro-ducers, and casting directors are turning away from the comedy of hipster racism and instead privileging colorblind *Cosby Show*–style humor that conforms to white middle-class heteronormative cultural tastes and social expectations.

The Turn Away from the Comedy of Hipster Racism

Unlike Obama's first presidential term, which was marked by a sense of colorblind optimism and racial progress, the second term of Obama's presidency (2012–16) was defined by deep ethnic and racial antagonisms and an effective assault on Civil Rights era policies and laws. A 2008 Pew Research Center study found that white, black, and Latino respondents held favorable opinions of one another and the relationships between them. In 2009, the year after Obama's election, a Pew Research Center poll found that 61 percent of the U.S. public across all ethnic and racial categories disagreed with the statement

"There hasn't been real improvement in the position of black people." By the end of Obama's presidency, views of racial inequality would dramatically change. A 2016 Pew Research Center study concluded: "Blacks, far more than whites, say black people are treated unfairly across different realms of life, from dealing with the police to applying for a loan or mortgage. And, for many blacks, racial equality remains an elusive goal." In sum, the study points to key differences in perceptions of inequality among ethnic and racial populations. While a small majority of white respondents (53 percent) believed the United States still had work to do to achieve equality, a large majority of African American respondents expressed concerns about the lack of equality and the possibility of ever achieving it. In another poll, the Pew Research Center (2017) concluded U.S. public attitudes about the state of race relations declined from a positive 44-percentage-point difference between those stating "generally good" and those stating "generally bad" in 2009 to a negative 4 percent difference in 2016.

As public attitudes about ethnicity, race, and minority–majority relations shifted from 2009 to 2016, the TV representational comedic landscape has also shifted. During this period, digital streaming television came of age, providing women, ethnic, racial, and sexual minorities with a more culturally and socially progressive platform on which to represent and be represented. In his work on digital peer-to-peer distribution, cultural producer and communications scholar Aymar Jean Christian (2014, 2018) documents the use of emerging digital platforms by ethnic, racial, and sexual minority producers to move beyond dominant representations of marginalized communities. Responding to political realities and technological pressures, by the end of Obama's presidential tenure TV comedies moved from the socially antagonistic colorblind comedy of hipster racism and the more progressive comedy of color or ethnic consciousness toward the socially safer middle ground of ethnic and racial minority acculturation to normative upper-middle-class whiteness.

Acculturation TV narratives harken audiences back to a nostalgic time when sitcoms featured ethnic and racial minority families, but ethnic and racial difference were not the central driver of the humor, narrative, or character development. For example, *Jane the Virgin* features the following characters: Jane (Gina Rodriguez), a second-generation Venezuelan woman who is accidentally artificially inseminated; Xiomara (Andrea Navedo), her hypersexualized single mother who dreams of being a famous entertainer; Rogelio (Jaime Camil), her newly discovered father who happens to be a famous telenovela star; and Alba (Ivonne Coll), her hyperreligious grandmother who refuses to speak English. Based on a Venezuelan telenovela, the show's ethnic specificity of the characters is background to the English-language adaptation's narrative of heterosexual romance, the dominant narrative that drives the storylines and character development. Similarly, *Black-ish* features a *Cosby Show*–style upper-middle-class family with a father, Dre (Antony Anderson), who wants to teach his economically entitled children about what it means to grow up black in the United States. The racial and class specificity of Dre's character as well as that of his biracial wife, Rainbow, who is a doctor, drives the comedy of errors. But many of the storylines engage that specificity to create humor out of the acculturation to white upper-middle-class heteronormative life. Narratives of acculturation, which tend to emphasize positive representations, do challenge dominant film and TV ethnic and racial stereotypes. Yet the storylines and the character development within these narratives also reinforce the feel-good colorblind ideology of white heterosexual normativity that underlies TV comedies.

Colorblind Comedy and the Anti-Latina Exotic

The production of laughter in acculturation sitcoms depends less on the ambiguous comedy of hipster racism and more on explicit comedic cues to signal socially appropriate laughter, such as wordplay, slapstick, and physical comedy. An example of the move away from hipster racism is Ferrera's character Amy in *Superstore*. Amy is written as the antiexotic Latina straight man in the spirit of Reyes's Carla or Nuñez's Oscar as defined in chapter 2. And like Plaza's April, the antiexotic Amy is situated in a colorblind comedic space where ethnicity and race inform the story's framework but not the narrative. Indeed, *Superstore* creator Justin Spitzer has writing credits on *Scrubs* and substantial production credits on *The Office*, whose creators also developed *Parks and Recreation*. Ferrera herself has directed episodes of *Superstore* and is part of the writers room for the show. Performing the role of a dispassionate assistant manager of a generic superstore, Ferrara was sought out by Spitzer to play the lead character, a working-class mother and part-time college student.

Managing the role of ethnic and racial difference in a colorblind comedic space is central to Amy's character development. The writers limit the amount of personal information that audiences learn about Amy. And Ferrera's nonstereotypical performance enhances the decision to minimize the ethnic context of Amy's identity. In the first season, Ferrera is typically costumed in the company's mandatory vest and work-friendly conservative attire typical of box stores like Walmart, which is the obvious referent for the show. Her makeup, hairstyle, and jewelry are kept to a minimum, emphasizing the everywoman nature of the role. Typical of female characters in TV shows, as the series progresses Ferrera's character is increasingly glamorized with more stylized makeup and hair (see figure 9). Like Plaza's straight-man performance in *Parks and Recreation*, everything about Ferrera's character is subdued. Her visual and verbal delivery is best defined as sarcastic, emotionless, and aggrieved. The character's name, Amy Dubanowski, lacks Latina or ethnic markers; and she speaks, like the second-generation actor who portrays her, in standard unaccented English. Audiences are not introduced to the fact that Amy has a daughter until the sixth episode ("Secret Shopper" 2016) and that she is married to a nonethnic white husband until the seventh episode ("Color Wars" 2016). It is not until the third episode of the series ("Shots and Salsa" 2015) that audiences are cued into Amy's Latina heritage, and audiences do not find out until the beginning of season two ("Olympics" 2016) that the character, like the actor, is of Honduran descent.

Similar to the analysis of *Parks and Recreation* in chapter 3, it is the stereotypic ethnic and racial assumptions of the white characters that are humorously called into question by *Superstore*'s writers. For instance, in "Shots and Salsa" Ferrera's comedic straight-man performance along with the producers' writing focus the narrative on the supervisor's assumptions about the need for a Latina/o employee to sell the company's salsa brand. However, it is done so in a manner that avoids creating a white character who is mean-spirited or reproducing ethnic and racial minority stereotypes. Amy, who identifies herself as Latina in this episode, refuses to market the store's generic

Figure 9. America Ferrera / *Superstore*

salsa or to obey managerial demands that she speak with an accent and wear a sombrero and poncho. She chastises the store's other Latina and gay Filipino characters for their willingness to do so. The script is as funny as it is smart. When Amy learns the salsa proceeds will go to a children's nonprofit organization, Ferrera's character overcomes her anger at the store's supervisors and finds herself wearing the sombrero and poncho and speaking with an accent. The development of Amy's character humorously creates the perception that life for white employers and ethnic and racial minority workers in the United States is complex but free from ethnic and racial conflict. Through its absent laugh track, colorblind casting, character development, and slapstick humor, the creators produce a storyline that makes it clear that the object of laughter is white corporate culture and its dependence on xenophobic, racist, sexist, and heteronormative retail practices. As a television reviewer for *The Atlantic* described the ethnic and racial humor on *Superstore*, it is "gloriously basic and uncomplicated" (Garber 2016). In typical colorblind fashion, the episode concludes with Amy's acknowledgment that it is impossible and perhaps undesirable to police ethnic and racial sensitivity or authenticity in the workplace. Playing the straight man on the show, at least through the first season, Ferrera's character is levelheaded, teetering on boring, in a workplace filled with zany and clownish characters.

Conclusion

After years of passing up television roles, Ferrera was called to perform the role of Amy precisely because of its difference from the usual employment of ethnicity and race on television: "[W]hen I saw how Justin was casting this show, it was a huge draw for me. None of the characters were written specifically for any race or ethnicity. The only one was Nico's character, who was written Mexican, and they cast a Filipino. We are so diverse, and we come from such different walks of life, and that was really exciting to me. I could see that Justin's vision, along with the other EPs, was to show a world that really reflected the world that we're living in" (Cohn 2015). Most television representations of Latina/o characters, such as those discussed in chapter 2, rely on the reproduction of familiar ethnic characteristics that stereotypically communicate Latina identity through the use of language, dress, or music, such as the use of Spanish, dance, or salsa music to signal Latina/o identity. In *Superstore* the producers develop Ferrera's performance of Amy to consciously work against audience expectations of traditional television performances of Latina identity, to produce a character who stands out for what she is not—a stereotypic or ethnic character. To return to the observations of Kristen Warner in the introduction of this book, *Superstore* is an example of colorblind casting and race-neutral feel-good TV programming that rejects the comedy of hipster racism.

Perhaps it was the call to ethnic specificity and color consciousness rather than the colorblind ethos of *Superstore* that led to the failure of its sister show *Telenovela*. Set behind the scenes of a Florida-based Spanish-language television production company, the show Longoria created was specifically situated in Latin American and U.S. Latina culture. Longoria performed the role of Ana, the stereotypical Latina lead of the telenovela *Pasión*—quick-tempered, heterosexual, voluptuous, feminine, and sexualized. Both the character and actor fit the physical, racial, and gender typecasting typical of starring female roles in most Spanish-language telenovelas (Rivero 2003). In doing so, Longoria played to and cleverly against the Latina spitfire type in her role as Ana.

However, the nuances of Ana's character rested in the actor who portrayed her. Neither Ana the character nor Longoria the actor are Latina spitfires. In an NBC.com interview promoting the show, Longoria, who starred in and executive-produced the series, remarked: "'I play the star, Ana Sofía, of a Spanish soap who does not speak Spanish—she just memorizes her lines, so she's kind of like a fish out of water," said Longoria, adding that's sort of how she grew up—a Texas Latina who didn't speak Spanish. Navigating that identity in the United States was definitely interesting. She said she has since learned Spanish and has a 'different relationship' with her heritage."

But Longoria the actor and Ana the character refused to live up to mainstream audience expectations about U.S. Latinas and Latina American stereotypes. Longoria is a politically active Hollywood celebrity. She fundraises for progressive political and social causes, and her political efforts have yielded speaking spots about Latina/o culture and civil rights at three Democratic presidential conventions (2008, 2012, 2016). Ana, the character created and performed by Longoria, used inserts to prop up her diminutive cleavage, hated spicy ethnic food, and did not enjoy nor know how to dance. Longoria, one of the most popular and commercially branded Latina actors on English-language television, cast herself in a role that specifically avoids hipster racism and disrupts the popular Latina stereotype she once performed on *Desperate Housewives* (2004–12). Instead, Longoria comically depicted an awkward character who was uncomfortable embodying her Americanized Mexican identity, an experience that personally resonates with the actor.[3]

As executive producer of *Devious Maids* (2013–16) and *Telenovela*, Longoria wanted to develop a new type of programming and intervention into Latina television representation, creation, and production:

> The other thing is, I knew if I was going back to comedy, I wanted to move the ball forward. You know, cable has really put pressure on dramas, but that pressure doesn't translate to comedies. I thought, "Comedies are comedies. There's nothing new." You know, the voice over was a certain device, and then there was the mockumentary of *The Office* and *Modern Family*, and that was a certain device. So what's the next new, fresh thing in comedy? And I thought this world. This is a world we haven't seen in television before. And that's what I knew I wanted to do when I went back to television. (Cohn 2015)

Rather than copying successful innovations in sitcom production that maintain the lives and social world of white heteronormative characters, Longoria wanted to foreground the ethnically specific experiences of U.S. Latina/o audiences. The comedy in *Telenovela* was an unabashedly satiric take on established Latina stereotypes in English- and Spanish-language programming, one that is much different than the English-language reiteration of the telenovela generic conventions found in *Jane the Virgin*. Instead, the show questioned the telenovela genre's and English-language sitcoms' dependence on recurring Latina/o stereotypes and traditional racial, gender, and sexual roles for Latina/o actors. The problem for the show was that to get the humor, one had to be familiar with both Latina television culture and the everyday politics of being a U.S. Latina.

The more complicated humor of *Telenovela* in which the writers sought to take apart English- and Spanish-language stereotypes about Latina/os and Latin Americans contributed to its failure. *Telenovela*'s writing, perhaps influenced by Longoria's role as executive producer, was too ethnically specific for non-Latina/o audiences. Much of the humor and the storylines depended on audiences' knowledge of the Spanish-language telenovela genre. More importantly, the humor depended on audiences' knowledge of the everyday experiences of U.S.-born Latina/o people in the United States. For example, one of the key recurring sources of comedy on the show was Longoria's character's inability to speak Spanish fluently. The joke depends on audiences' ability to relate to the experiences of generations of U.S.-born Latina/os, many of whom are non-Spanish speakers. Audiences were invited to empathize with and see themselves through Ana's experience of having others (fans, television executives, etc.) deploy language to discipline her identity as authentically Latina. It is a linguistic experience that speaks to Longoria's specific history and the reality of generations of U.S.-born Latina/os. The joke was potentially humorous to U.S. Latina/os because it spoke to the everyday. But to non-Latina/o audiences the series' premise that Ana's character could barely speak Spanish was simply funny because she starred in a Spanish-language television show. This became the problem for the producers of *Telenovela*. Non-Latina/o audiences may not have been familiar with Spanish-language telenovela conventions or the nuances of U.S.-born Latina/o identity. The producers overestimated the ability or willingness of non-Latina/o audiences to relate to the ethnically specific experiences of a character so different from their own experiences. *Telenovela*'s characters were more difficult to love, the humor was a little harder to grasp, and the feel-good elements of the comedy were easier to parody for audiences not familiar with the complexities of contemporary U.S.-born Latina/o identity.

Feel-Good Comedy: A Response to the Comedy of Hipster Racism

In the context of the post-racial era of comedy outlined in this book, the most telling characteristic of *Modern Family, Parks and Recreation, Superstore,* and *Telenovela* is the nostalgic return to feel-good comedy during Obama's second term. Comedies in the Trump era are moving further away from hipster racism and toward humor with less ethnically and racially charged context. The tone of many comedies provides audiences with a moment of escapism (from the widening wealth gap; state sanctioned violence against black, brown, and queer people; and the 2015 campaign and 2016 election of Donald J. Trump) through the production of feel-good stories and characters. *Telenovela,* for example, poked fun at the soap genre by finding humor in the deconstruction of the genre's stereotypes and celebrating typical sitcom storylines of friendship and romance. The producers of *Superstore* cast a nationally beloved Latina actor to play the antiexotic lead in a colorblind multicultural ensemble show about social misfits negotiating the contemporary blue-collar labor system, a system in which workers in the United States increasingly find themselves. Both shows produce an all-American feel-good comedic narrative. Mimicking the success of *Parks and Recreation,* the producers of *Telenovela* and *Superstore* developed characters whose innate moral goodness is easy for audiences to love and consciously moved away from the racially, sexually, and ethnically offensive comedy of hipster racism discussed in chapter 2. Given Spitzer's insistence on comparing the show to *The Office* in a Walmart setting, *Superstore*'s producers could have easily copied the successful comedic formula of *The Office.* The producers could have used the mockumentary formula and hipster racism to pit white resentment and the implicit racial, ethnic, and sexual biases of the manager against the multicultural experiences of the floor workers. *Superstore* did not.

What Does the Future of Television Promise for Latina/os?

Post-racial comedic writing takes advantage of the usually white lead characters and audiences' racial, ethnic, gender, and sexual prejudices discussed in chapter 2. Ethnic, racial, sexual, and gender biases are deployed in the scripts through plays on hipster racism. However, beginning in 2014, contemporary TV comedy is increasingly negotiating the everyday complexities of race, gender, and sexuality by developing a multicultural ensemble of likeable and relatable characters, often through colorblind casting, and placing those characters in universally familiar and relatable situations without the social edge of *The Office* or *Modern Family* outlined in chapter 3. Instead of hipster racism, the leading white actors of TV comedies deliver racist, sexist, or homophobic lines with a type of social innocence that compels audiences' forgiveness, empathy, and intercultural understanding, what entertainment journalist Megan Garber (2016) refers to as basic, easy, uncomplicated television. There is little ambiguity about the source of social offense or the well-meaning behavior of the offender. The comedy is uncomplicated and simple.

As discussed in the introduction, the minimal yet increased visibility of Latina/o characters on TV comedies across all platforms (broadcast, subscription, and streaming) is ultimately an economic strategy, a strategy that creates the market appearance of progressive inclusion while still ignoring the ethnic and racial structural inequalities of TV production and everyday life in the United States (Castañeda 2014). In a critique of the contemporary politics surrounding media representations, Herman Gray (2013) concludes that demands by cultural activists for increases in multicultural representations actually contribute to the continued erasure of gender and racial inequalities. Latina/o actors and characters on comedic programming function as a form of "neoliberal multiculturalism" (Melamed 2011). Neoliberal multiculturalism manages the contradictions of ethnic and racial life in the United States by producing the appearance of equity. Audiences perceive increased visibility of and desirability for Latina bodies in the media (Báez 2014). Yet ethnic, racial, and gender identity remains devalued in the cultural, political, and social sphere. By celebrating incremental steps in screen visibility, legacy and digital media leave ethnocentrism, racism, and sexism within the entertainment industry and society largely unchallenged. Cultural representation becomes a visible sign of social progress contributing to the erasure of continuing social and economic barriers for ethnic and racial minorities in the United States (López and Patten 2015).

Despite demographic and consumer trends, English-language legacy and digital media have remained slow to buy into "Latino spin," the rhetoric used by Latina/o politicians and media marketers to assert that the Latina/o population is powerful and profitable or soon will be (Dávila 2008). Instead the approach used by legacy and digital U.S. television executives and producers toward Latina/o audiences remains defined by language biases and pan-ethnic stereotypes, such as assumptions that the Latina/o population is Spanish dominant and prefers to consume media in Spanish (Chávez 2015). Industry reports actually point to the complexity of Latina/o audiences. For instance, second- and third-generation Latina/o audiences tend to be English dominant and are more likely to consume English-language content across a variety of platforms. The 2015 *Advertising Age Hispanic Fact Pack* documented that more than 60 percent of Latina/o audiences watch television programming completely or mostly in English. Nielsen findings also show that, unlike black viewers, who are more likely to watch programming with black actors and characters, Latina/o audiences generally follow white viewership trends. For example, in 2013 *Monday Night Football, The Voice, Modern Family*, and *Scandal* were among the top ten shows for Latina/o viewers (Advertising Age 2014). In 2016 Fox's *Empire* (2015–Present) and NBC's *Shades of Blue* (2016–Present), featuring Latina character Harlee Santos (Jennifer Lopez), made it to the top thirty-five for Latina/o viewers (Media Life 2016). The success of shows like *Modern Family* and *Superstore* reflect the networks' continuing biases in developing English-language shows that target white and wealthier mainstream audiences and use multicultural casting to expand young ethnic and racial audience demographics.

For many entertainment journalists, the addition of diverse comedic programming filled with ethnically and racially diverse ensemble casts might signal that such diversity is finally here to stay. As discussed throughout the book, the continuing lack of diversity behind the camera of these shows demands a more sobering celebration. In the end, the television programs explored in this book, as do the majority of legacy and digital TV shows featuring multicultural ensemble casts, remain someone else's vision about what it is like to live ethnic and racial minority lives in the United States, an outsider's sense of what is funny or socially appropriate to laugh at with regard to Latina/os. Advertisers and network programmers remain committed to a young, wealthy, and presumably white consumer, even as those advertisers and programmers are increasingly aware of the economic potential of a less wealthy but much larger demographically diverse audience base.

While this book is concerned with good or bad, positive or negative representations of Latina/os or other ethnic and racial minorities on television or elsewhere in the media, a greater concern is the need for ethnic and racial minority characters and storylines to be shaped by ethnic and racial minority writers and creators. By calling for more creative diversity, the claim is not that there is some essential or authentic experience of ethnic and racial minority life that can or should be represented in the media. Rather, attention should be placed on the cultural and social risk of gender and racial homogeneity among television executives, creators, and writers. Greater diversity behind the camera is necessary for generating creativity in front of the camera that breaks away from established and traditional genres, stereotypes, and archetypes and moves audiences beyond what we are already comfortable and familiar with. For Aymar Jean Christian (2018) one solution to the lack of production and content by creative workers of color is to invest in independent peer-to-peer production and distribution. As access to high-speed internet and smartphone technology increases, such TV platforms are increasingly viable. Television in all of its forms (legacy and digital) is here to stay. It is thus important for communication and media scholarship to study the representational and for journalists and audiences to become more critically literate of the media content that is consumed.

Post-racial discourses and values in the media, legal courts, and by U.S. citizens are increasingly under attack. Black Lives Matter activists, undocumented student activists, and activists opposed to Trump's populist agenda, among other groups, highlight the power of visual and rhetorical discourse to contest the symbolic environment. Communications scholars Michael Lacy and Kent Ono (2011) propose that critical scholarship and education regarding representations of ethnicity and race in the media are a significant type of political intervention. Helping audiences to "see" race and ethnicity and their intersections with gender and sexuality produces an understanding of how the representations and the conditions of production and reception of those representations are linked to social and political life. Developing a critical literacy toward comedic TV depictions of ethnic and racial minority life does indeed matter.

NOTES

Introduction

1. I use the following terminology in the book: "Latinidad" references the pan-ethnic use of cultural signifiers commonly used by the media to signal Latina/o and Latin American identity. "Latina/o" and "Latina/o American" are used as pan-ethnic, gender-specific terms to describe people who are, either by ancestry or immigration, living in the United States. Latina/o scholarship recognizes the unique historical, linguistic, gender, and racial experiences of specific ethnic groups within the pan-ethnic umbrella. I refer to characters and actors by using ethnic-specific labels such as Cuban, Dominican, Mexican, or Colombian. While I recognize the great diversity within each category, non-Latina/o populations in the United States will be referenced through racial labels such as black and white or ethnic labels such as Asian, African, and Italian.

2. Primetime television viewing is defined by the Nielsen Company as the period between 8 and 11 p.m., Monday through Friday. With digital recording and on-demand technology allowing audiences to tune in to programming on their individual schedules and mobile devices, Nielsen now includes time-shifted ratings into its calculation of total audience viewership of primetime programs.

3. Adherence to the belief that racism is an individual rather than a structural problem underlies responses by mostly white U.S. citizens to issues such as racially discriminatory policing practices, for instance.

Chapter 1

1. Like other sitcoms in production during the September 11th attacks, *Scrubs* did not textually reference the attacks. *Friends*, which is set in New York City, received the most backlash for its decision to ignore the event.

2. *The Office*, which was also filmed with one camera, moved out of a real office space after the first season and into a complete sound studio reproduction of the original office space.

3. The writers room is the physical space where the showrunner, executive producers, and other writers on the show gather to conceive the stories.

4. As a point of contrast *The Office*'s only credited producer or writer of color was the Indian American actress Mindy Kaling. That said, Kaling served as a primary producer and writer for the show, producing 128 of *The Office*'s 187 episodes. And as a result of her success with *The Office*, she became the showrunner for her own program, *The Mindy Project* (2012–Present). *The Office* production team also encouraged the cast, which was mostly made up of stand-up comedians, to participate in the direction and production of the show.

5. Potential advertisers as well as trade and entertainment journalists are provided a "first look" at television shows scheduled to premiere in a given year. As a result of the feedback from the first looks, network executives may demand changes to the program, determine the place of a show in the lineup, or extend the production contract for a series.

6. Quoted from published script.

7. Dialogue and actions transcribed by the author.

8. Published script and additional notations by author.

9. Reyes is a founding member of the LAByrinth Theatre Company, a multicultural acting space in Manhattan.

Chapter 2

1. While no one set of elements characterizes the mockumentary (mock documentary) as a film or television genre, in this book it is defined as the comedic use of documentary practices and devices to comically represent a fictional world as a reflection of the "real" (Hight 2010).

2. Margaret Cho's *All American Girl* (1994) premiered on ABC. The unconventional show challenged Asian American stereotypes critiquing white heterosexual privilege. It was the first sitcom to star an Asian American character/actor.

3. According to the latest FBI Crime Statistics, hate crimes are trending downward except for anti-Muslim hate crimes and LGBTQ hate crimes since 2013 (Federal Bureau of Investigation 2015). The majority of hate crimes victims (59.2%) were targeted because of ethnicity, race, or ancestry.

4. Although on different networks, both programs overlapped between 2009 and 2013.

5. *Scrubs* was continually moved around on NBC's programming schedule, and after NBC canceled the show, it moved to ABC.

6. Published script for "Diversity Day," September 14, 2004.

7. The term was actually coined for Vélez's portrayal in the "Mexican Spitfire" movies.

8. According to the Gay & Lesbian Alliance Against Defamation's 2012 *Media Report*, Oscar's character was the only gay person of color on television when the show aired in 2005 and one of only a handful when the show's run ended in 2013.

9. Recognizing the humorous possibilities, the producers provided audiences with knowledge of the character's gay identity while keeping it from the other characters until the third season. The producers may have kept the character closeted longer if they did not need to write Nuñez temporarily off the show, so he could pursue his own independent television project.

Chapter 3

1. Mike Schur would help Aziz Ansari and Alan Yang create Netflix's critically acclaimed *Master of None*.

2. Levitan was an executive producer on *Stacked* (2005–6), a workplace sitcom featuring Anderson.

Conclusion

1. The book does not analyze comedies outside of ABC, CBS, and NBC.

2. I thank research assistant Morten Kristensen for pointing out this irony.

3. Played by Latina/o or Latin American actors, the other characters on the show also broke Spanish- and English-language media stereotypes in interesting ways. Jose Moreno Brooks played Gael, *Pasión*'s hypermasculine heterosexual love interest who actually was Ana's queer offscreen friend. And the telenovela's villain, performed by Afro-Latino actor Amaury Nolasco, was a sentimental and emotionally sensitive lover off screen.

REFERENCES

Adalian, Josef. 2001a. "TV Sitcom Train Jumps Laugh Track." *Variety*, February 26: 1, 62.
———. 2001b. "First Look: 'Scrubs.'" *Variety*, September 14: A18.
Adalian, Josef, and Rick Kissell. 2001. "Nets Draw Fall Battle Lines." *Variety*, August 7: 13.
Advertising Age. 2014. *Hispanic Fact Pack 2014.*
———. 2015. *Hispanic Fact Pack 2015.*
Amaya, Hector. 2013. *Citizenship Excess: Latinas/os, Media, and the Nation.* New York: New York University Press.
Aranda-Mori, Ayre. 2014. "Mobile Movie Marketing—Ideal Medium to Connect with Influential Latinos." *Reach Hispanic*, April 8.
Arredondo, Gabriella. 2008. *Mexican Chicago: Race, Identity, and Nation, 1916–39.* Urbana: University of Illinois Press.
Báez, Jillian. 2014. "Latina/o Audiences as Citizens: Bridging Culture, Media, and Politics." In *Contemporary Latina/o Media: Production, Circulation, Politics*, edited by Arlene Dávila and Yeidy Rivero, 267–84. New York: New York University Press.
Béltran, Mary. 2005. "The New Hollywood Racelessness: Only the Fast, Furious, (And Multiracial) Will Survive." *Cinema Journal* 44 (2): 50–67.
———. 2008. "Mixed Race in Latinowood: Latino Stardom and Ethnic Ambiguity in the Era of Dark Angel." In Béltran and Fojas, *Mixed Race Hollywood*, 248–68.
———. 2010. *Latina/o Stars in U.S. Eyes: The Making and Meaning of Film and TV Stardom.* Champaign: University of Illinois Press.
Béltran, Mary, and Camilla Fojas, eds. 2008. *Mixed Race Hollywood.* New York: New York University Press.
Berg, Charles Ramírez. 2000. *Latino Images in Film: Stereotypes, Subversion, Resistance.* Austin: University of Texas Press.
Berg, Madeline. 2017. "Full List: The World's Highest-Paid TV Actors and Actresses 2017." *Forbes.* Published September 28. https://www.forbes.com/sites/maddicberg/2017/09/28/full-list-the-worlds-highest-paid-tv-actors-and-actresses-2017/#66ba9cc71725.
Bonilla-Silva, Eduardo, and Austin Ashe. 2014. "End of Racism? Colorblind Racism and Popular Media." In *The Colorblind Screen: Television in Post-Racial America,* edited by Sarah Nilsen and Sarah. E. Turner, 57–82. New York: New York University Press.
Burns, Ashley and Chloe Schildhause. 2015a. "You Go Big or You Go Home: An Oral History of The Creation and Evolution Of 'Parks and Recreation.'" Uproxx. Published February 23. http://uproxx.com/feature/parks-and-recreation-evolution-oral-history/.
———. 2015b. "The Behind-the-Scenes Story of 'Diversity Day': The Episode That Defined NBC's 'The Office.'" Uproxx. Published March 23. http://uproxx.com/feature/feature-the-behind-the-scenes-story-of-diversity-day-the-episode-that-defined-nbcs-the-office/2/.
Cacho, Lisa Marie. 2012. *Social Death: Racialized Rightlessness and the Criminalization of the Unprotected.* New York: New York University Press.
Carter, Bill. 2001. "TV Seeks Normalcy in Troubled Times: A Disrupted Premiere Week Dawns with Comedy and Familiarity Flavored." *New York Times*, September 24.
Calafell, Bernadette Marie. 2012. "Monstrous Femininity: Constructions of Women of Color in the Academy." *Journal of Communication Inquiry* 36: 111–30.
Cantor, Brian. 2014. "ABC's 'Blackish' Nearly Matches Its 'Modern Family' Lead-In." *Headline Planet*, September 24.

Carini, Susan. 2003. "Love's Labors Almost Lost: Managing Crisis during the Reign of 'I Love Lucy." *Cinema Journal* 43 (1): 44–62.

Castañeda, Mari. 2014. "The Role of Media Policy in Shaping the U.S. Latino Radio Industry." In *Contemporary Latina/o Media: Production, Circulation, Politics*, edited by Arlene Dávila and Yeidy Rivero, 186–205. New York: New York University Press.

Cepeda, Maria Elena. 2010. *Musical ImagiNation: U.S.–Colombian Identity and the Latin Music Boom*. New York: New York University Press.

Chavez, Leo. 2001. *Covering Immigration: Popular Images and the Politics of the Nation*. Berkeley: University of California Press.

———. 2013. *The Latino Threat: Constructing Immigration, Citizens, and the Nation*. Redwood City, Calif.: Stanford University Press.

Chávez, Christopher. 2015. *Reinventing the Latino Television Viewer: Language Ideology and Practice*. Lanham, Md.: Lexington Books.

Christian, Aymar Jean. 2014. "Indie TV: Innovation in Series Development." In *Media 3 Independence: Working with Freedom or Working for Free?*, edited by James Bennett and Niki Strange, 159–81. New York: Routledge.

———. 2018. *Open TV: Innovation Beyond Hollywood and the Rise of Web Television*. New York: New York University Press.

Cohn, Paulette. 2015. "America Ferrera on Why *Superstore* Lured Her Back to Series TV." *Parade*, December 31. http://parade.com/447466/paulettecohn/america-ferrera-on -why-superstore-lured-her-back-to-series-tv/.

———. 2015. "Eva Longoria Talks about Her Return to TV in NBC's Flashy Comedy *Telenovela*." *Parade*, December 31. https://parade.com/447046/paulettecohn/eva -longoria-talks-her-return-to-tv-in-nbcs-flashy-comedy-telenovela/.

Dávila, Arlene M. 2001. *Latinos, Inc.: The Marketing and Making of a People*. Berkeley: University of California Press.

———. 2008. *Latino Spin*. New York: New York University Press.

Del Rio, Esteban. 2006. "The Latina/o Problematic: Categories and Questions in Media Communication Research." In *Communication Yearbook 30*, edited by Christina S. Beck, 387–429. Mahwah, N.J.: Lawrence Erlbaum.

Doane, Ashley. 2014. "Shades of Colorblindness: Rethinking Racial Ideology in the United States." In *The Colorblind Screen: Television in Post-Racial America*, edited by Sarah Nilsen and Sarah E. Turner, 15–38. New York: New York University Press.

Dunn, Jancee. 2011. "Sofía Vergara Spills All: The Smurfs and Modern Family Star Opens Up about Being a Young Mom and Surviving Divorce and Cancer." *Redbook*, August 15. http://www.redbookmag.com/life/interviews/a12370/Sofía-vergara-interview/.

Enck-Wanzer, Darrel. 2011. "Barack Obama, the Tea Party, and the Threat of Race: On Racial Neoliberalism and Born Again Racism." *Communication, Culture, Critique* 4: 23–30.

Esposito, Jennifer. 2009. "What Does Race Have to Do with *Ugly Betty*? An Analysis of Privilege and Postracial (?) Representations on a Television Sitcom." *Television and New Media*, 10 (6): 521–35.

Federal Bureau of Investigation. 2016. "Annual Report Sheds Light on Serious Issue." Federal Bureau of Investigation. Published November 14. https://www.fbi.gov/news/ stories/2015-hate-crime-statistics-released.

Fernández, Lilia. 2012. *Brown in the Windy City: Mexicans and Puerto Ricans in Postwar Chicago*. Chicago: University of Chicago Press.

Felts, Susannah. 2011. "Scrubs Star Judy Reyes: Give Nurses the Props They Deserve." *Health*. Published April 27. http://www.health.com/health/article/0,,20411643,00.html.

Fiske, John. 1996. *Media Matters: Everyday Culture and Political Change*. Rev. ed. Minneapolis: University of Minnesota Press.

Fregoso, Rosa Linda. 2003. *MeXicana Encounters: The Making of Social Identities on the Borderlands*. Berkeley: University of California Press.

Freeman, Michael. 2001. "Nets Narrow Down Pilot Choices." *Electronic Media*, May 7.

Garber, Megan. 2016. "The Joys of Basic Television." *The Atlantic*, January 5. http://www.theatlantic.com/entertainmentarchive/2016/01in-praise-of-mediocre-television/422691/.

Genzlinger, Neil. 2016. "Review: 'Superstore' and 'Telenovela' Play It Safe on NBC." *New York Times*, January 4.

Gillota, David. 2013. *Ethnic Humor in Multiethnic America*. New Brunswick, N.J.: Rutgers University Press.

Gitlin, Todd. 2000. *Inside Primetime*. Berkeley: University of California Press.

GLAAD. 2012. "Where We Are on TV: Media Report." GLAAD. Published October 4. http://www.glaad.org/files/whereweareontv12.pdf.

Gonzalez, Eva. 2014. "Engaging the Evolving Hispanic Consumers: Look at Two Distinct Subgroups." Nielsen Company. Published September 25. http://www.nielsen.com/us/en/insights/news/2014/engaging-the-evolving-hispanic-consumers.html.

Gordon, Avery, and Christopher Newfield. 1996. "Introduction." In *Mapping Multiculturalism*, edited by Avery Gordon and Christopher Newfield, 1–18. Minneapolis: University of Minnesota Press.

Gray, Herman. 1994. *Watching Race: Television and the Struggle for Blackness*. Minneapolis: University of Minnesota Press.

———. 2013. "Subject(ed) to Recognition." *American Quarterly* 65 (4): 771–98.

Gray, Jonathan. 2008. *Television Entertainment*. New York: Routledge.

Hall, Stuart. 1985. "Althusser and Post-Structuralist Debates." *Critical Studies in Mass Communication* 2: 91–114.

———.1986. "Gramsci's Relevance for the Study of Race and Ethnicity." *Journal of Communication Inquiry* 10 (2): 5–27.

———. 1992. "Race, Culture, and Communications: Looking Backward and Forward at Cultural Studies." *Rethinking Marxism* 5 (1): 10–18.

———. 1997. *Representation: Cultural Representations and Signifying Practices*. London: Sage in association with the Open University.

Halterman, Jim. 2014. "The New TV Gay Character: Just One of the Guys on NBC's 'Undateable.'" Xfinity. Published June 4. http://my.xfinity.com/blogs/tv/2014/06/04/the-new-tv-gay-character-just-one-of-the-guys-on-nbcs-undateable.

Harvey, David. 2005. *A Brief History of Neoliberalism*. Oxford: Oxford University Press.

Heisler, Steve. 2009. "Bill Lawrence." AV Club. Published May 6. https://tv.avclub.com/bill-lawrence-1798216490.

Hight, Craig. 2011. *Television Mockumentary: Reflexivity, Satire and a Call to Play*. London: Manchester Press.

Hunt, David, Ana-Christina Rámon, and Zachary Price. 2014. *2014 Hollywood Diversity Report: Making Sense of the Disconnect*. Report by the Ralph Bunche Center for African American Studies at UCLA. Los Angeles: University of California Los Angeles.

———. 2015. *Hollywood Diversity Report: Flipping the Script*. Report by the Ralph Bunche Center for African American Studies. Los Angeles: University of California Los Angeles.

Hunt, David, Ana-Christina Rámon, and Michael Tran. 2016. *Hollywood Diversity Report: Busine$$ as Usual*. Report by the Ralph Bunche Center for African American Studies. Los Angeles: University of California Los Angeles.

———. 2017. *Hollywood Diversity Report: Setting the Record Straight*. Report by the Ralph Bunche Center for African American Studies. Los Angeles: University of California Los Angeles.

IMDb. n.d. "Judy Reyes." Accessed June 17, 2016. http://www.imdb.com/name/
   nm0721332/?ref_=nv_sr_1.
Inside the Actors Studio. Season 17, Episode 5, "The Cast of Modern Family." Aired June 1,
   2011, on Bravo.
Jhally, Sut, and Justin Lewis. 1992. *Enlightened Racism: The Cosby Show, Audiences, and
   the Myth of the American Dream.* Boulder, Colo.: Westview Press.
Kang, Cecilia. 2015. "With Shows Like 'Empire,' 'Black-ish' and 'Cristela,' TV Is More
   Diverse Than Ever." *Washington Post,* January 29.
King, C. Richard. 2014. "Watching TV with White Supremacists: A More Complex
   View of the Colorblind Screen." In *The Colorblind Screen: Television in Post-Racial
   America,* edited by Sarah Nilsen and Sarah E. Turner, 219–36. New York: New York
   University Press.
Kissel, Rick. 2013. "ABC Leads Premiere Ratings in Affluent Younger Viewers." *Variety,*
   October 2.
Kloer, Phil. 2003. "From Dark 'Angel' to Hip-Hop 'Honey.'" *Cox News Service,* November
   12.
Kuryla, Peter. 2011. "Barack Obama and the American Island of the Color Blind." *Patterns
   of Prejudice* 45 (1–2): 119–132.
Kteily, Nour, and Emile Bruneau. 2017. "Backlash: The Politics and Real-World
   Consequences of Minority Group Dehumanization." *Personality and Social
   Psychology Bulletin* 43 (1): 87–104. https://doi.org/10.1177/0146167216675334.
Lacy, Michael, and Kent Ono, eds. 2011. *Critical Rhetorics of Race.* New York: New York
   University Press.
Law & Order. Season 2, Episode 17, "Sisters of Mercy." Directed by Fred Gerber and writ-
   ten by Rene Balcer. Aired March 3, 1992, on NBC.
Lawrence, Bill. 2001. "Scrubs (pilot)." Accessed November 4, 2016. http://www
   .simplyscripts.com/tv_rs.html.
Levitan, Steven, and Christopher Lloyd. 2008. "Pilot." *Modern Family: My American
   Family.* Revised Second Draft.
Lipsitz, George. 1990. *Time Passages: Collective Memory and American Popular Culture.*
   Minneapolis: University of Minnesota Press.
López, Ana. 1991. "All Latins from Manhattan? Hollywood, Ethnography, and Cultural
   Colonialism." In *Unspeakable Images: Ethnicity and the American Cinema,* edited by
   Lester D. Friedman, 404–24. Champaign: University of Illinois Press.
———. 2000. "Early Cinema and Modernity in Latin America." *Cinema Journal* 40 (1): 48–78.
López, Gustavo, and Eileen Patten. 2015. "The Impact of Slowing Immigration: Foreign-
   Born Share Falls Among 14 Largest U.S. Hispanic Groups." Pew Research Center.
   Published September 15. http://www.pewhispanic.org/2015/09/15/the-impact-of
   -slowing-immigration-foreign-born-share-falls-among-14-largest-us-hispanic-origin
   -groups/.
Lotz, Amanda. 2004. "Textual (Im)Possibilities in the U.S. Post-Network Era: Negotiating
   Production and Promotion Processes on Lifetime's Any Day Now." *Critical Studies in
   Media Communication* 21 (1): 22–43.
Loza, Mireya. 2016. *Defiant Braceros: How Migrant Workers Fought for Racial, Sexual,
   and Political Freedom.* Chapel Hill: The University of North Carolina Press.
Markert, John. 2004. "'The George Lopez Show': The Same Old Hispano?" *Bilingual
   Review* 28 (2): 148–65.
Mateo, Ashley. 2010. "Sofía Vergara Reveals Her True Self." *Self,* October 14. https://www
   .self.com/gallery/sofia-vergara-slideshow.
Mayer, Vicky. 2011. *Below the Line: Producers and Production Studies in the New
   Television Economy.* Durham, N.C.: Duke University Press.

Medialife. 2015. "Hispanic TV: It Goes Beyond Language. TV Preferences Vary Widely by
Generation. It's Also Cultural." *Medialife*, October 22. http://www.medialifemagazine
.com/hispanic-tv-more-than-spanish-language/.

———. 2016. "The Top English-Language Shows with Hispanics." *Medialife*, April 7.
http://medialifemagazine.com/the-top-english-language-shows-with-hispanics/.

Melamed, Jody. 2011. *Represent and Destroy: Rationalizing Violence in the New Racial
Capitalism*. Minneapolis: University of Minnesota Press.

Mendible, Myra. 2007. "Introduction: Embodying Latinidad: An Overview." In *From
Bananas to Buttocks: The Latina Body in Popular Film and Culture*, edited by Myra
Mendible, 1–28. Austin: University of Texas Press.

Menjívar, Cecilia. 2011. "The Power of the Law: Central Americans' Legality and Everyday
Life in Phoenix, Arizona." *Latino Studies* 9 (4): 377–95.

———. 2014. "Immigration Law Beyond Borders: Externalizing and Internalizing Border
Controls in an Era of Securitization." *Annual Review of Law and Social Science* 10:
353–69.

———. 2016. "Immigrant Criminalization in Law and the Media: Effects on Latino
Immigrant Workers' Identities in Arizona." *American Behavioral Scientist* 60 (5–6):
597–616.

Menjívar, Cecilia, and Leisy J. Abrego. 2012. "Legal Violence: Immigration Law and
the Lives of Central American Immigrants." *American Journal of Sociology* 117 (5):
1380–1421.

Menjívar, Cecilia, and Sarah M. Lakhani. 2016. "Transformative Effects of Immigration
Law: Immigrants' Personal and Social Metamorphoses through Regularization."
American Journal of Sociology 121 (6): 1818–55. https://doi.org/10.1086/685103.

Mills, Brett. 2008. *Television Sitcom*. London: British Film Institute.

———. 2009. *The Sitcom*. Edinburgh: Edinburgh University Press.

Mitchell, Amy, and Dan Page. 2015. *State of the News Media 2015*. Washington, D.C.: Pew
Research Center.

Mittell, Jason. 2015. *Complex TV: The Poetics of Contemporary Television Storytelling*.
New York: New York University Press.

Mock, Erin Lee. 2011. "The Horror Of 'Honey, I'm Home!': The Perils of Postwar Family
Love in the Domestic Sitcom." *Film & History* 41 (2): 29–50.

Modern Family. Season 1, Episode 1, "Pilot." Directed by Jason Winer and written by
Steven Levitan and Christopher Lloyd. Aired September 23, 2009, on ABC.

———. Season 1, Episode 2, "The Bicycle Thief." Directed by Jason Winer and written by
Bill Wrubel. Aired September 30, 2009, on ABC.

———. Season 1, Episode 3, "Come Fly with Me." Directed by Reginald Hudlin and written
by Dan O' Shannon. Aired October 7, 2009, on ABC.

———. Season 1, Episode 4, "The Incident." Directed by Jason Winer and written by
Steven Levitan. Aired October 14, 2009, on ABC.

———. Season 1, Episode 5, "Coal Digger." Directed by Jason Winer and written by
Christopher Lloyd. Aired October 21, 2009, on ABC.

———. Season 1, Episode 6, "Run for Your Wife." Directed by Jason Winer and written by
Paul Corrigan and Brad Walsh. Aired October 28, 2009, on ABC.

———. Season 1, Episode 9, "Fizbo." Directed by Jason Winer and written by Paul
Corrigan and Brad Walsh. Aired November 25, 2009, on ABC.

———. Season 1, Episode 10, "Undeck the Halls." Directed by Randall Einhorn and written
by Dan O' Shannon. Aired December 9, 2009, on ABC.

———. Season 1, Episode 12, "Not in My House." Directed by Chris Koch and written by
Caroline Williams. Aired January 13, 2010, on ABC.

———. Season 1, Episode 18, "Starry Night." Directed by Jason Winer and written by Danny Zuker. Aired March 24, 2010, on ABC.

———. Season 2, Episode 6, "Halloween." Directed by Michael Spiller and written by Jeffrey Richman. Aired October 27, 2010, on ABC.

———. Season 4, Episode 3, "Snip." Directed by Gail Mancuso and written by Danny Zuker. Aired October 10, 2012, on ABC.

———. Season 4, Episode 5, "Open House of Horrors." Directed by James R. Bagondas and written by Elaine Ko. Aired October 24, 2012, on ABC.

———. Season 4, Episode 12, "Party Crasher." Directed by Fred Savage and written by Danny Zuker and Christopher Lloyd. Aired January 16, 2013, on ABC.

———. Season 4, Episode 13, "Fulgencio." Directed by Lev L. Spiro and written by Bill Wrubel. Aired January 16, 2013, on ABC.

———. Season 4, Episode 19. "The Future Dunphys." Directed by Ryan Case and written by Elaine Ko. Aired April 3, 2013, on ABC.

———. Season 6, Episode 22. "Patriot Games." Directed by Alisa Statman and written by Vali Chandrasekaran. Aired April 3, 2013, on ABC.

———. Season 8, Episode 2. "A Stereotypical Day." Directed by Ryan Case and written by Vali Chandrasekaran. Aired September 28, 2016, on ABC.

Molina-Guzmán, Isabel. 2010. *Dangerous Curves: Latina Bodies in the Media*. New York: New York University Press.

———. 2013. "Ethnoracial Ambiguity in Post-Racial Televisual World." In *Latinos and Narrative Media: Participation and Portrayal*, edited by Frederick Luis Aldama, 143–60. New York: Palgrave.

Molina-Guzmán, Isabel, and Angharad Valdivia. 2004. "Brain, Brow or Bootie: Latina Iconicity in Contemporary Popular Culture." *Communication Review* 7 (2): 203–19.

Moreno, Carolina. 2016. "America Ferrera and Eva Longoria Reveal Who Wrote Their Golden Globes Bit." *Huffington Post*. Modified December 29. http://www .huffingtonpost.com/entry/america-ferrera-and-eva-longoria-reveal-who-wrote-their -golden-globes-bit_us_56992257e4b0ce496424323d?ir=Entertainment&section= entertainment&utm_hp_ref=entertainment.

Morgan, Michael, James Shanahan, and Nancy Signorielli, eds. 2012. *Living with Television Now: Advances in Cultivation Research and Theory*. New York: Peter Lang.

Morreale, Joanne. 2003. *Critiquing the Sitcom*. Syracuse, N.Y.: Syracuse University Press.

Motel, Seth, and Eileen Patten. 2012. "Hispanics of Columbian Origin in the United States, 2010." Pew Research Center. Published June 27. http://www.pewhispanic.org/ 2012/06/27/hispanics-of-colombian-origin-in-the-united-states-2010/.

National Latino Media Council. 2014. "Annual Television Network Diversity Report: 2013–2014." National Latino Media Council. Published September 8.

Negron-Muntañer, Frances, with Chelsea Abbas, Luis Figueroa, and Samuel Robson. 2014. *The Latino Media Gap: A Report on the State of Latinos in US Media*. New York: Center for the Study of Ethnicity and Race.

Nielsen Company. 2012. "State of the Media: Advertising and Audiences Part 2: By Demographics." Nielsen Company. Published April 27. http://www.nielsen.com/ content/dam/corporate/us/en/reports-downloads/2012-Reports/nielsen-advertising -audiences-report-spring-2012.pdf.

———. 2014. "Content Is King, but Viewing Habits Vary by Demographic." Nielsen Company. Published December 3. http://www.nielsen.com/us/en/insights/news/ 2014/content-is-king-but-viewing-habits-vary-by-demographic.html.

Noriega, Chon. 2000. *Shot in America: Television, the State, and the Rise of Chicano Cinema*. Minneapolis: University of Minnesota Press.

Oboler, Suzanne. 1995. *Ethnic Labels, Latino Lives: Identity and the Politics of (Re)
Presentation in the United States*. Minneapolis: University of Minnesota Press.

———. 2006. "Redefining Citizenship as a Lived Experience." In *Latinos and Citizenship:
The Dilemma of Belonging*, edited by Suzanne Oboler, 3–30. New York: Palgrave
McMillan.

Ono, Kent, and John Sloop. 2002. *Shifting Borders: Rhetoric, Immigration, and California's
Proposition 187*. Philadelphia: Temple University Press.

Paley Center. 2002. "Television Festival 2002." Los Angeles, March 8.

———. 2010. "PaleyFest." Los Angeles, February 26.

———. 2015. "PaleyFest." Los Angeles, March 14.

Pardo, Claudia and Charles Dreas. 2011. "The Things You Thought You Knew About US
Hispanic Engagement with Media and Why You May Be Wrong." Nielsen Company.
http://www.nielsen.com/content/dam/corporate/us/en/newswire/uploads/2011/04/
Nielsen-Hispanic-Media-US.pdf.

Paredez, Deborah. 2010. *Selenidad: Selena, Latinos, and the Performance of Memory*.
Durham, N.C.: Duke University Press.

Park, Jane Chi Hyun. 2014. "The Failure of Asian American Representation in *All-
American Girl* and *The Cho Show*." *Gender, Place and Culture: A Journal of Feminist
Geography*, 21 (5): 637–49.

Parks and Recreation. Season 2, Episode 5, "Sister City." Directed by Michael Schur and
written by Alan Yang. Aired October 15, 2009, on NBC.

———. Season 6, Episode 1, "London: Part 1." Directed by Dean Holland and written by
Michael Schur. Aired September 26, 2013, on NBC.

Patten, Eileen. 2016. "The Nation's Latino Population Is Defined by Its Youth." Pew
Research Center. Published April 20. http://www.pewhispanic.org/2016/04/20/the
-nations-latino-population-is-defined-by-its-youth/.

Patton, Tracy. 2004. "In the Guise of Civility: The Complicitous Maintenance of
Inferential Forms of Sexism and Racism in Higher Education." *Women's Studies in
Communication* 27 (1): 60–87.

Pew Research Center. 2009a. "Hispanics in the News: Events Drive the Narrative." Pew
Research Center Reports. Published December 7. http://www.journalism.org/2009/
12/07/hispanics-news/.

———. 2009b. "Section 5: Social and Political Attitudes About Race." U.S. Politics & Policy.
Published May 21. http://www.people-press.org/2009/05/21/section-5-social-and
-political-attitudes-about-race/.

———. 2015. "State of the News Media 2015." Pew Research Center. Published April 29,
2015. http://assets.pewresearch.org/wp-content/uploads/sites/13/2017/05/30142603/
state-of-the-news-media-report-2015-final.pdf.

———. 2016. "On Views of Race and Inequality, Blacks and Whites Are Worlds Apart."
Pew Social Trends. Published June 27. http://www.pewsocialtrends.org/2016/06/27/
on-views-of-race-and-inequality-blacks-and-whites-are-worlds-apart/.

———. 2017. "Public Opinion on Race Relations, 1990–2016." Pew Research Center.
Published January 10. http://www.pewresearch.org/interactives/public-opinion-on
-race-relations-1990-2016/.

Pieracinni, Christina, and Douglass Alligood. 2005. *Color Television: Fifty Years of African
American and Latino Images on Prime Time Television*. Dubuque, Iowa: Kendall/
Hunt Publishing Co.

Porter, Rick. 2015. "Broadcast Weekly Top 25: 'Sunday Night Football' Leads, 'Empire'
Tops Scripted Shows for Nov. 9–15." TV by the Numbers. Published November 17.
http://tvbythenumbers.zap2it.com/weekly-ratings/broadcast-weekly-top-25-nov-9
-15-2015/.

Ramirez-Berg, Charles. 2000. *Latino Images in Film: Stereotypes, Subversion, Resistance*. Austin: University of Texas Press.

Reddit. 2015. "Why Does Everyone Hate Carla So Much?" Accessed December 15, 2015. https://www.reddit.com/r/Scrubs/comments/3cuftz/why_does_everyone_hate_carla _so_much/.

Rivero, Yeidy. 2003. "The Performance and Reception of Televisual 'Ugliness' in *Yo soy Betty la fea*." *Feminist Media Studies* 3 (1): 65–81. doi:10.1080/14680770303793.

———.2005. *Tuning Out Blackness: Race and Nation in the History of Puerto Rican Television*. Durham, N.C.: Duke University Press.

Rodriguez, Clara. 1997. *Latin Looks: Images of Latinas and Latinos in the U.S. Media*. Boulder, Colo.: Westview Press.

———. 2000. *Changing Race: Latinos, the Census and the History of Ethnicity*. New York: New York University Press.

———. 2008. *Heroes, Lovers, and Others: The Story of Latinos in Hollywood*. New York: Oxford University Press.

Rowles, Dustin. 2014. "The Behind-the-Scenes 'Divorce' That Changed 'Modern Family' Forever and Drives Its Dueling Personalities." Uproxx. Published November 20. http://uproxx.com/tv/the-behind-the-scenes-divorce-that-drives-the-dueling-personalities -of-modern-family/.

Salcido, Olivia, and Cecilia Menjívar. 2012. "Gendered Paths to Legal Citizenship: The Case of Latin-American Immigrants in Phoenix, Arizona." *Law and Society Review* 46 (2), 335–68. https://doi.org/10.1111/j.1540-5893.2012.00491.x.

Santa Ana, Otto. 2002. *Brown Tide Rising: Metaphors of Latinos in Contemporary American Public Discourse*. Austin: University of Texas Press.

———. 2012. *Juan in a Hundred: The Representation of Latinos on Network News*. Austin: University of Texas Press.

Saraiya, Sonia. 2015. "NBC Finally Gets the Diversity Memo: Jennifer Lopez, Eva Longoria and America Ferrera Head 3 Very Different Shows Aimed at Latina Viewers." Salon. Published January 15. https://www.salon.com/2016/01/15/nbc _finally_gets_the_diversity_memo_jennifer_lopez_eva_longoria_and_america_ferrera _head_3_very_different_shows_aimed_at_latina_viewers/.

Savorelli, Antoni. 2010. *Beyond Sitcom: New Directions in American Television Comedy*. Jefferson, N.C.: McFarland.

Scrubs. Season 1, Episode 1, "My First Day." Directed by Adam Bernstein and written by Bill Lawrence. Aired October 2, 2001, on NBC.

———. Season 1, Episode 3, "My Best Friend's Mistake." Directed by Adam Bernstein and written by Eric Weinberg. Aired October 9, 2001, on NBC.

———. Season 3, Episode 1, "My Own American Girl." Directed by Bill Lawrence and written by Bill Lawrence. Aired October 2, 2003, on NBC.

———. Season 6, Episode 6, "My Musical." Directed by Will Mackenzie and written by Debra Fordham. Aired January 18, 2007, on NBC.

Sheridan, Patricia. 2006. "Patricia Sheridan's Breakfast with Judy Reyes." *Pittsburgh Post-Gazette*, March 20.

Smith, Stacy, Marc Choueiti, and Katherine Pieper. 2014a. *Race and Ethnicity in 600 Popular Films: Examining on Screen Portrayals and Behind the Camera Diversity*. Los Angeles: Media Diversity and Social Change Initiative at the USC Annenberg School for Communication.

———. 2014b. *Gender Inequality in Popular Films: Examining on Screen Portrayals and Behind-the-Scenes Employment Patterns in Motion Pictures Released 2007–2013*. Los Angeles: Media Diversity and Social Change Initiative at the USC Annenberg School for Communication.

———. 2015. *Race and Ethnicity in 600 Popular Films: Examining on Screen Portrayals and Behind the Camera Diversity*. Los Angeles: Media Diversity and Social Change Initiative at the USC Annenberg School for Communication.

———. 2016. *Inclusion & Invisibility? Gender, Media, Diversity & Social Change Initiative*. Los Angeles: Media Diversity and Social Change Initiative at the USC Annenberg School for Communication.

———. 2017. *Inequality in 900 Films*. Los Angeles: Media Diversity and Social Change Initiative at the USC Annenberg School for Communication.

Spigel, Lynn, and Michael Curtin, eds. 1997. *The Revolution Wasn't Televised: Sixties Television and Social Conflict*. New York: Routledge.

Spigel, Lynn, and Denise Mann, eds. 1992. *Private Screenings: Television and the Female Consumer*. Minneapolis: University of Minnesota Press.

Squires, Catherine. 2012. "Coloring in the Bubble: Perspectives from Black-Oriented Media on the (Latest) Economic Disaster." *American Quarterly* 64 (3): 543–70.

———. 2014. *The Post-Racial Mystique: Media & Race in the Twenty-First Century*. New York: New York University Press.

Steel, Emily. 2015. "How Is US TV Changing? Ask Jane." *New York Times*, May 10.

Sue, Derald Wing, Christina M. Capodilupo, Gina C. Torino, Jennifer M. Bucceri, Aisha M. B. Holder, Kevin L. Nadal, and Marta Esquilin. 2007. "Racial Microaggressions in Everyday Life: Implications for Clinical Practice." *American Psychologist* 62 (4): 271–86.

Sullivan, John. 2015. "Leo C. Rosten's Hollywood: Power, Status, and the Primacy of Economic and Social Networks in Cultural Production." In *Production Studies: Cultural Studies of Media Industries*, edited by Vicki Mayer, Miranda Banks, and John T. Caldwell, 39–53. New York: Routledge.

Superstore. Season 1, Episode 3, "Shots and Salsa." Directed by Ruben Fleischer and written by Justin Spitzer. Aired December 28, 2015, on NBC.

———. Season 1, Episode 6, "Secret Shopper." Directed by Alex Hardcastle and written by Lon Zimmet. Aired January 18, 2016, on NBC.

———. Season 1, Episode 7, "Color Wars." Directed by Andy Ackerman and written by Jack Kukoda. Aired January 25, 2016, on NBC.

———. Season 2, Episode 1, "Olympics." Directed by Ruben Fleischer and written by Jonathan Green. Aired August 19, 2016, on NBC.

Tanamor, Jason. 2009. "Oscar Nunez of NBC's 'The Office' Is the Gayest Straight Man on Television." Zoiks! Online. Published November 3. http://www.zoiksonline.com/2009/11/oscar-nunez-of-nbcs-office-is-gayest.html.

The Office. Season 1, Episode 2, "Diversity Day." Directed by Ken Kwapis and written by B.J. Novak. Aired March 29, 2005, on NBC.

———. Season 3, Episode 1, "Gay Witch Hunt." Directed by Ken Kwapis and written by Greg Daniels. Aired September 21, 2006, on NBC.

Torres, Maria de los Angeles. 2003. *The Lost Apple: Operation Pedro Pan, Cuban Children in the U.S., and the Promise of a Better Future*. Boston: Beacon Press.

Tsuruoka, Sonia. 2012. "Character Studies: April, *Parks and Recreation*." Slate. Published April 19. http://www.slate.com/blogs/browbeat/2012/04/19/april_ludgate_played_by_aubrey_plaza_is_the_best_character_on_parks_and_recreation.html.

TV by the Numbers. 2010. "Guess the Ratings for Premiere Wednesday: 'Modern Family,' 'Law & Order: SVU,' 'The Defenders' & Many More." TV by the Numbers. Published September 22. http://tvbythenumbers.zap2it.com/broadcast/guess-the-ratings-for-premiere-wednesday-modern-family-law-order-svu-the-defenders-many-more/.

Turow, Joseph. 1978. *Getting Books to Children: An Exploration of Publisher-Market Relations*. Chicago: American Library Association.

———. 1984. *Media Industries: The Production of News and Entertainment*. New York: Longman.

———. 2000. "Segmenting, Signaling and Tailoring: Probing the Dark Sides of Target Marketing." In *Critical Studies in Media Commercialism*, edited by Robin Andersen and Lance Strate, 239–49. New York: Oxford University Press.

Uffalussy, Jennifer Gerson. 2015. "Why Are Latino Viewers the Most Important for Networks?" *The Guardian*, January 1. https://www.theguardian.com/tv-and-radio/tvandradioblog/2015/jan/01/why-are-latino-viewers-important-for-networks.

Warner, Kristen. 2015. *The Cultural Politics of Colorblind TV Casting*. New York: Routledge.

Whalen, Carmen, and Victor Vázquez-Hernández, eds. 2005. *The Puerto Rican Diaspora: Historical Perspectives*. Philadelphia: Temple University Press.

Wilson, Charles, Felix Gutierrez, and Linda Chao. 2012. *Racism, Sexism, and the Media: Multicultural Issues New Communications Age*. Thousand Oaks, Calif.: Sage.

Wojcik, Pamela R. 2003. "Typecasting." *Criticism* 45 (2): 223–49.

Valdivia, Angharad. 2000. *A Latina in the Land of Hollywood and Other Essays on Media Culture*. Tucson: University of Arizona Press.

———. 2004. "Latinas as Radical Hybrid: Transnationally Gendered Traces in Mainstream Media." *Global Media Journal* 4 (7).

———. 2008. "Mixed Race on the Disney Channel: From *Johnny Tsunami* through *Lizzie McGuire* and Ending with *The Cheetah Girls*." In Béltran and Fojas, *Mixed Race Hollywood*, 269–89.

———. 2010. *Latina/os in the Media*. London: Polity.

Vargas, Lucilla. 2000. "Genderizing Latino News: an Analysis of a Local Newspaper's Coverage of Latino Current Affairs." *Critical Studies in Media Communication* 17 (3): 261–93.

———. 2009. *Latina Teens, Migration, and Popular Culture*. New York: Peter Lang.

INDEX

Note: Television and film characters are alphabetized by first name, with the name of the actor playing them in parentheses. Page numbers in italics represent illustrations.

Index

135

Stonestreet, Eric, 48, 98–99, 99–101
Superstore (2015–Present), 22, 103, 108–10

Telenovela (2015–16), 103, 112–13, 121
Terri Alden (Priscilla Barnes, *Three's Company*), 32–33
The Cosby Show (1984–92), 7, 50
The Office (2005–13), 23–24, 29, 47, 48, 52–63, 119, 120
Tom Haverford (Aziz Ansari, *Parks and Recreation*), 86. *See also* Ansari, Aziz
transgender people. *See* LGBTQ people
transphobia, 99
Trump, Donald J., 66, 82, 113
Turk (Donald Faison, *Scrubs*), 29–30, 41–42
TV production. *See* production practices
typecasting, 16–17, 18–20. *See also* casting

Vergara, Sofía: accent and physical appearance of, 18, 67, 68, 69–71, 73 (*see also*

"Latin look"); as Gloria in *Modern Family* (*see* Gloria); income and endorsements of, 3, 49; Lucille Ball as role model for, 65; performance skills of, 64–65, 79, 89, 101

Wallace, Pierce, 96
Warner, Kristen, 5, 8, 10, 54, 59
whiteness, 33–40, 59, 78–80, 98–102
Winston, Randall, 29–30
World War II, 64
Wright, Aloma, 36–38
writers, 10–12, 19, 66–67, 86, 116–17, 119. *See also* specific individuals; specific shows

Xiomara (Andrea Navedo, *Jane the Virgin*), 90, 107

Yang, Alan, 85

ABOUT THE AUTHOR

ISABEL MOLINA-GUZMÁN is an associate professor of media and cinema studies and Latina/o studies and the associate dean of the Graduate College at the University of Illinois at Urbana-Champaign. She served as chair of the Department of Latina/Latino Studies in 2007–2008 and 2009–13. Her research involves the study of ethnic, racial, and gender inequality in news and entertainment media with a focus on Latina/os. She is the author of *Dangerous Curves: Latina Bodies in the Media* (NYU Press, 2010). Her work has appeared in numerous edited collections and academic journals, including *Latino Studies, Journalism,* and *Popular Communication,* and she is currently on the editorial boards of publications such as *Critical Studies in Media Communication* and *Feminist Media Studies.*